Creative Learning Practices:
European Experiences

the Tufnell Press,
London,
United Kingdom

www.tufnellpress.co.uk

email contact@tufnellpress.co.uk

British Library Cataloguing-in-Publication Data
A catalogue record for this book is
available from the British Library

ISBN 1872767 575
Copyright © 2006   Bob Jeffrey
The moral rights of the authors have been asserted.
Database right the Tufnell Press (maker).

First published 2006

Printed in England and USA by Lightning Source

Creative Learning Practices: European Experiences

edited by
Bob Jeffrey

Acknowledgements

The Creative Learning and Students' Perspectives research project (CLASP) was part funded (€250,000) by the European Commission's Socrates programme (No. 200-4682/002-001, SO2 610 BGE) from December 2002 until October 2004 for a total period of nine months. The United Kingdom Economic and Social Science Research Council (ESRC) part funded (£34,000) the co-ordination and the UK partner's project. Each of the ten partner universities also part funded their own research project.

We would also like to acknowledge the invaluable assistance given by Dr. Geoff Troman, of Roehampton University, who acted as methodological consultant to the whole project and to The Open University's administrative and finance departments for acting as contract holder and supporting the co-ordinator Bob Jeffrey of the same institution. Our thanks also go to Professor Peter Woods of The Open University for the tutelage and collegiality provided over the ten years before the commencement of the project and his encouragement in persuading us to venture into Europe and develop our research. Further thanks go to Anna Craft, also of The Open University, for general support in this area of research and to Lisbeth Laing for much work on the project, including this collection. Lastly, the ten European partners of the project deserve commendation for their professionalism, collegiality and creativity. Without their enthusiasm, dedication and commitment this project would have failed.

Contents

International background

The policy context for the the Creative learning and Student Perspectives was a situation across Europe in which education was seen as the cornerstone of a knowledge-based society, one that encompassed the principle of life-long learning (OECD 2002) and where two significant policy discourses were and still are at the centre of this principle. An international discourse highlights the importance of creativity (Craft et al. 2001) across economic, industrial, government and educational arenas. It notes that creativity is eminently suited to the multiple needs of life in the twenty first century (Seltzer and Bentley, 1999), which calls for skills of adaptation, flexibility, initiative and the ability to use knowledge on a different scale than has been hitherto realised. As manufacturing began to disperse globally in the latter part of the twentieth century, space was created for new forms of wealth production through increased marketing, the growth of service industries, electronic communications and e-commerce market—the 'weightless economy' (op. cit.). Work patterns are also undergoing a revolution in that there is an increased demand for more highly educated, motivated employees who are able to use more autonomy in applying skills in combination with flexible technology and work processes. Although qualifications are still integral to personal success, it is no longer enough for students to show that they are capable of passing public examinations. To thrive in our economy, defined by the innovative application of knowledge, we must be able to do more than absorb and feedback information (op. cit.)

Alongside the creativity policy discourse there is a global interest in raising educational achievement levels to benefit future economic development by increasing the skills base and having an educated workforce who fit the requirements of the knowledge economy and an emphasis on performance-based assessment is a major strategy of this policy. These policies are linked to the creation of a culture of performativity (Lyotard, 1979; Ball, 1998; Ball, 2000), a principle of governance that enables strictly functional relationships to develop between a state and its inside and outside environments over and against the older policy technologies of professionalism and bureaucracy through the institutionalisation of new management techniques and the development of 'mutual instrumentalism' (Ball, 2003; Pollard et al. 2000; Yeatman, 1994; Whitty and Edwards, 1998). Performativity is a technology, a culture and mode of regulation that employs judgements, comparisons and displays as a means of incentive, control, attrition and change. The incentives are based on material and symbolic rewards and sanctions where the performances of individual subjects or organisations serve as measures of productivity, displays of 'quality' or 'moments' of promotion or inspection. As such they stand for, encapsulate or represent the worth, quality or value of an individual or organisation within a field of judgement. In short, two complex related policy agendas are discernible in 'the heat and noise of reform' (Ball, 1998, p. 125) and their relationships in ten different education systems was the background to the research upon which this edited collection is based.

The CLASP Project

The broad objectives of the Creative learning and Student Perspectives (CLASP) were:

+   to identify teachers' and students' strategies for developing creative learning in educational contexts.

+   to examine the effectiveness of incorporating student perspectives into the teaching and learning process.

+   to highlight the advantages to be gained for the quality of teaching and learning by examining cross European creative pedagogic practices.

The innovative nature of the project lay in combining two cross-national policy developments, an interest in the expansion of creativity and the effectiveness gained from incorporating student perspectives into pedagogic practices. The combination is reciprocal in that developing creative learning enhanced creative practices and encouraged student commitment.

The research sites for this project varied but the number of schools was kept to a minimum to fulfil the requirements of the project to produce full qualitative analysis over time with a small sample using ethnographic methods. The target groups were students, from age three upwards, and teachers in a maximum of three teaching and learning contexts in each of the ten participating countries.

The target groups for dissemination were schools, head teachers and policy advisors at a local level, educational researchers, policy advisers and student organisations at a macro level.

The main activity was qualitative research for nine months involving fieldwork observations, conversations, interviews with teachers and pupils and development work concerned with creative learning in the educational sites. This was interspersed with regular electronic communication and meetings with partners to compare, research, record and evaluate our critical analyses, research data and process. The researchers acted as participant observers to interpret contexts and situations and to engage in dialogues with teachers and students concerning their research analysis. Digital photographs were collected as data and used to stimulate discussion and debate with teachers and students. Students were informed of the study's aims and objectives and encouraged to take roles as researchers (Raggl and Schratz, 2004). Ethnographic methodology is a 'bottom up', grounded approach, which first locates the empirical cases, taking care to specify the criteria by which they are selected, and then employs a range of theories to portray and explain them' (Woods, 1996, p. 11). As a collaborative cross-national project, we needed a discourse through which to communicate a relevant set of common lenses with which to conduct our fieldwork. Although these lenses were specific to this project they can be easily adapted to other projects using a similar methodology (Troman and Jeffrey, 2005).

The co-ordinating partner was The Open University and the main co-ordinator of the project was Bob Jeffrey, Research Fellow of The Open University.

The partners to this project were:

Austria	Department of Teacher Education and School Research, University of Innsbruck
Belgium	Catholic University of Professional Education of South West Flanders, Kortrijk (Uncompleted project)
Denmark	The Danish Institute for Upper Secondary Education, University of Southern Denmark, Odense
England	The Faculty of Education and Language Studies, The Open University, Milton Keynes
Ireland	St. Patrick's College, Dublin City University
Poland	Academy of Humanities and Economics, Lodz
Portugal	Faculty of Sciences /Department of Education, University of Lisbon.
Scotland	Department of Primary Education, University of Strathclyde, Glasgow
Spain	Department of Education, University of Cadiz.
Sweden	Department of Education, Göteborg University

This Open University research project was funded by the European Commission—Socrates Project—Action 6. 1 'General activities of observation and analysis with a grant of €549, 000. We were one of only eight projects funded in 2002 and the average award across the partners was approximately €55, 000. However, this particular programme only funded partner projects with 45.48% of grant as the European Commission expected each educational institutional to match the balance in order to show their commitment to the specific research area. The Final Report was approved in April 2005.

Those benefiting most from the study were students and student organisations, teachers, head teachers, teacher trainers, policy advisors and academics who used the reports to promote student representation, to improve the quality of learning practices in schools and colleges, raise student commitment, develop national, local and institutional creative learning policies, and increase understanding of creative learning. Researchers on the project also benefited as they built a European discourse on creative learning, education in general and education in other countries.

Partner policy contexts
National and local

The national contexts show a significant amount of national and/or local policy change taking place in all the partner countries that affected the subject of this research—creative learning. However, these changes are not necessarily all in one direction or of a similar nature. It is clear that each of the countries represented in the research have different starting points for change.

According to the partner reports new national discourses and policies relating directly to creative and more flexible curriculum programmes have been introduced in the last few years in Denmark, England, Ireland, Portugal, Sweden and Scotland. These vary in extent, influence and character, for example: England has extensively incorporated creativity criteria across its national curriculum programmes and funded a national programme of arts and education projects and Portugal has designated part of the school week to include student interests. Ireland renewed its commitment to child-centred education albeit in an individualised form and focused at the same time on achievement levels but Social, Personal and Health Education and Drama was elevated from being a good pedagogical vehicle for learning to the status of a fully-fledged subject in its own right. Denmark has national programmes for youth and upper secondary age that demand integrated curriculum project work and looser and more flexible programmes have been introduced in Scotland where the New National Priorities include the encouragement of 'creativity and ambition'. In Sweden and Denmark there has been a national new educational vision that describes shared responsibility and a local appropriation of national policy declarations as central for education in the future. It emphasises an increase in delegated responsibilities to the learner (and the local arena more generally), self-determination and freedom of choice for the students who are exhorted to create their own knowledge. However, control in Sweden and Denmark has shifted from steering by rules and directives to steering by objectives and results in which a different relationship to learning is expressed. Learners are now described in national policy texts in Sweden as creative, self-reliant and discerning consumers and producers of knowledge and it is the job of schools and teachers to eliminate all obstacles that currently stand in the way of them exercising their skills and capabilities to the full (Beach, 2004; Beach and Dovemark, 2005b; Borgnakke 2004, forthcoming; Dovemark 2004a; Dovemark 2004b)

We can also report that where there are national initiatives for creative teaching and learning they have generally been placed on top of existing policies of assessment and performativity and in some cases have not materialised as was intended—Dublin, Glasgow and Gothenburg. In Dublin they introduced a new national curriculum alongside new assessment programmes and professional development programmes. These created tensions for schools and teachers as they tried to incorporate new policies, which in some cases conflicted with contemporary policies and practices. The Odense schools, having incorporated new IT-based strategies for teaching and learning, nevertheless used a traditional mix of teaching styles e.g. the classic lecture, the classroom teacher directed style as well as student directed group work and project work.

In Glasgow the emphasis was on achievement and attainment and there was little room for creativity except in the arts and physical education though there were also programmes on learning for life which included references to encouraging creativity as an ambition. This added to the workload and increased dilemmas and tensions. In Gothenburg, as indicated above, there have been national reforms to increase flexible learning and open schooling. However, the school buildings themselves did not lend themselves to this policy and nor did the level of staffing which needed to be increased to deal with more individualised programmes of learning. Consequently, the experience of teachers and student alike was of contradictory policies and experiences resulting in alienation from their own creativity and their own productive life.

Teachers and students had to accept overload if they wished to maintain some creative teaching and learning programmes. They struggled to incorporate them alongside the testing and competitive regimes, a task in which many succeeded (Ireland, England, Portugal, and Scotland). The justification for continual support for non creative learning experiences from the perspectives of teachers and students was the necessity for students to purchase credits for future work opportunities (Ireland, England, Portugal, Scotland, and Sweden) but there were signs that some partners were managing to incorporate creative learning into performativity programmes (Denmark, Ireland, England, Poland, and Scotland).

To summarise, we found evidence of teacher excitement, uncertainty, anxiety, a loss of professionalism and re-professionalisation in national and local reforms of educational priorities for learning. Some partners experienced policy requirements as demanding but they also experienced a release of creative teaching, e.g. Odense, Lodz and Lisbon. Others found opportunities more limited, e.g. Gothenburg.

In spite of the tensions found in these examples it is clear that schools and teachers also manipulated the situation to ensure that their educational values concerned with creative teaching and learning were maintained and in some cases they found that they were able to claim a 'redress of creativity' for themselves and for their schools. The Milton Keynes schools made use of Government funds available for arts and education to develop large school based projects. Teachers used the Scottish programmes, which funded the development of a multi-lingual teaching involving asylum seekers, to engage in teaching that was more creative. In spite of the problem of overload the Dublin research schools used the formal introduction of constructivist policies to legitimate their own pedagogies based in this area of teaching and they felt freer to experiment with ideas such as the transformation of space (see below). The Lisbon research sites took full advantage of the national programme to plan a week of project work and a day of exhibitions and presentations in costume by the students and the Glasgow group challenged their students to plan and fund an outing in response to a curriculum imperative to learn about their environment. The Cadiz schools did something similar with secondary students by encouraging them to document on computer, and in presentations, the biology and history of their environment and one of the Innsbruck schools created an adventure school environment for the students to explore. All these local appropriations give an indication of how schools and teachers enhanced the quality of learning for their students by adapting national programmes to suit the local context. They, creatively, also found ways of reconstructing the programmes to show how they might be developed in different ways to those anticipated by policy makers.

Social and intellectual objectives

As the project progressed we discovered additional social and intellectual objectives emanating from the institutions and teachers, e.g.: developing autonomy decision making and risk taking (Lisbon); the social development of learners and respect for their perspectives (Odense); ownership of space and relationship responsibility and social obligations to classroom democratic practices, role play and empathy (Cadiz and Innsbruck); the promotion of participatory practices (Lisbon, Milton Keynes, Cadiz, Innsbruck, Odense, Lodz, and Glasgow). However, we also found stratification practices (Gothenburg). Intellectual objectives were achieved by: encouraging possibility thinking, and providing open adventures, open tasking and solution seeking problems as well as intellectual risk taking (Milton Keynes); interdisciplinary project work involving extensive problem solving (Odense and Lisbon). However, constructivist principles, on which much of this teaching and learning was based, were also seen as a barrier to performativity imperatives (Gothenburg).

The papers in this volume represent firstly attempts by institutions and teachers to reconstruct performativity programmes or to provide authentic creative teaching and learning programmes through the implementation of critical events and specialist programmes. In particular, the papers from Cadiz, Innsbruck, Milton Keynes, Glasgow, Odense, Lisbon and Gothenburg represent these factors. Secondly, the articles show the influence of these programmes on relationships between teachers, between teachers and students and between students and in particular the chapters from Cadiz, Innsbruck, Glasgow, Dublin, Odense, Gothenburg and Lodz exemplify this theme. Thirdly, they show the extent to which the students themselves saw the programmes as successful e.g. the chapters from Innsbruck, Milton Keynes, Glasgow, Dublin, Lisbon, Gothenburg and Lodz. These student perspectives were a central element of the CLASP project.

Edited collection themes

Teacher strategies and influences

The research sites were schools and colleges and the policies of these schools and their teachers were crucial to the development of creative learning contexts and experiences. In the main the schools and teachers were the instigators of the specific school and class creativity programmes and they determined the processes by which creative learning was experienced by students. They were also the people who, together with the influence of resources and community partners, constructed the quality of the creative learning environments in which the students worked.

One of the major strategies across most of the partners' reports was the instigation of 'real' programmes, similar to 'critical events', (Woods 1993) that were designed to both effect the interest and commitment of students but also to influence institutional and local area policy. These 'real' programmes had, according to the students, a social and educational reality that legitimised their involvement as social beings. There were school environment improvements and analysis (Milton Keynes and Cadiz), coordinated international projects (Odense), computer toy constructions for major competitions (Dublin), business case studies (Lodz), re-enactments of social issues and local histories (Cadiz, Gothenburg, and Lisbon) and the examination of lives from different cultures (Glasgow). These events either were in place of the designated curriculum or incorporated into an existing programmes and usually enhancing it. For example, designating specialist weeks to a particular curriculum subject right across the school, (Milton Keynes) and the allocation of a specific week to a creative project (Lisbon, Cadiz, Odense, Glasgow, and Lodz) They also often involved strategic co-operations with external partners and organisations in the community such as dancers, artists, sculptors, actors, environmental workers (Gothenburg, Milton Keynes and Innsbruck,).

Their creativity programmes conformed to the structure of a critical event, which goes through well-defined stages of conceptualisation, preparation and planning, divergence, convergence, consolidation, and celebration (Woods 1993). The Innsbruck school, as indicated above, prepared the outside environment, with the help of the community as a physical adventure for learners in which curriculum programmes were enacted. The environment was used for learning and stories were told outside. One of the classes in a Dublin school was transformed into a classroom in Victorian times where the children used slates and worked in silence for the day (Sugrue 2004a) and in the Odense school, the learners worked on a virtual project concerning the Middle Ages. They worked on the project with learners in Iceland and Norway via internet communications. The Lodz adult learners were given management case studies to investigate in groups for a number of teaching sessions and in an unusual twist the students and the lecturer examined the teaching and learning through videos and meetings and together devised negotiated pedagogies. The Lisbon project culminated in a day when all the students dressed up as some of the historical characters they had been investigating in groups and they experienced carnival day. In one of the Cadiz Early Years schools the learners regularly held cultural events such as weddings, divorces, and celebratory meals, initiations such as baptisms, confirmations and differing cultural equivalents. As indicated above the Glasgow learners raised funds for an outing to a well known beauty spot by making and selling cakes and having fairs, booking their own coaches, tours, organising lunches and marketing the outing as well as the learning activities for the day. One of the Milton Keynes schools had a maths and a design and technology week where the whole school focused on a particular theme within these subjects. The week's events included visits to local zoos, football clubs, pizza parlours and other schools and specialists were employed to run large workshops in the school hall or grounds or in the kitchens. Another Milton Keynes school planned a 'sounds in the environment' programme lasting weeks, one class worked with the National Theatre for two terms, another with a specialist dance teacher and a whole school was engaged in renovating the school environment with the help of artists, sculptors and community workers.

The results of these activities were similar to Peter Woods' (1993) experiences of critical events. He found that the 'outcomes for learners included positive attitudes to learning, new found confidences, motivation for learning, enhanced disposition, and skills in listening to others and being listened to, self discovery, realisation of abilities and interests, a 'coming out' of a new found self, blending in to previous impenetrable cultures and emotional development' (ibid, see chapter five).

The decision by these schools to create a critical event established a special time period, or project within the school timetable, which in some cases was integrated within the rest of the curriculum programme. In others, they were treated separately, although they often involved the use of other curriculum subjects or directly influenced separate subject study. The critical event also involved a considerable amount of external engagement from advisors, artists, specialist funders, workshop providers, project specialists and visits.

A second major factor in establishing a creative learning climate and a commitment from students was teacher enthusiasm and dedication. Formal professional development in IT practices and team teaching was felt necessary in the Odense project and it led to many collaborative practices between teachers and between teachers and students. Alternatively, in the Dublin research sites, creative teaching was seen as a gift and particular teachers were praised for their strategic use of humour, imagination, inventiveness and the ability to merge the formal and informal. In other projects teachers played a vital role as a facilitator and chairperson who modelled respect for everyone's opinions and valued peer learning and insisted on alerting student's to other's authentic labour (Cadiz). They also modelled themselves as students and observers (Innsbruck) as moderators (Lisbon) and they acted creatively in looking for spaces between the dominating discourses of performativity and ineffective top down policies of flexible learning (Gothenburg).

Influences on relationships

A particular outcome of these creative teaching and learning strategies were changes in relationships and innovative developments in interactive engagements. Participatory practices and experiences were observed across the partners but the Lisbon paper, in particular, emphasised the affective and teacher-student relations. The Glasgow project emphasised relevant teacher strategies for the bilingual learners with whom they were engaged as they brought the environment and local culture into the classroom as well as exploring it *in situ*. The Odense project specifically focused on teacher participatory strategies and encouraged relations with other foreign cultures expecting students to collaborate in investigations. One result of this was the support given by the students to teachers in their dispute over teaching cuts through a student strike. The emotional labour exhibited by teachers resulted in higher levels of trust and an exchange of skills took place between teachers and students (Dublin). Young children were encouraged to play a full part in daily democratic decision-making and take responsibility for those decisions at the expense of themselves and in support of others and collective decision-making. They developed relationships by solving their own disputes and closer home and school relations brought a holistic environment to learning (Cadiz). A major feature of the Innsbruck research site was parents as partners, peer assistance and collaborations between parents, teachers and students acting as co-creators. A different form of close relationship was analysed in the Gothenburg study, that of mutual instrumentalism between teachers and learners to meet external and institutional learning targets. The study examines the consequences of a breakdown of relations for working class students in situations where those with cultural capital dominated relationship space.

Student evaluations

A major part of the CLASP project was to gain some evaluations of the student's learning experiences. The Lisbon project achieved a critical analysis from learners and recognition of peer abilities as well as the development of feelings of belonging from the students. The Glasgow project with bilingual learners showed how they had developed a 'multi-lingual conference' as the basis for creative learning and the general findings from Odense was that the project work carried out by the students and the new relationships established with teachers led to a firmer commitment from students. Students from the Cadiz project evaluated their activities daily, both in terms of how they worked and details of pleasure and discomfort. However, where the learning was not particularly creative or meaningful students tended to blame themselves rather than the school system.

This collection of papers in this volume represents the CLASP research in institutions from early years to adult education including special classes and are published in that order.

References

Ball, S.J. (1998) Performativity and fragmentation in 'Postmodern Schooling', in Carter, J. (ed.) *Postmodernity and Fragmentation of Welfare,* London, Routledge

Ball, S.J. (2000) Performativities and Fabrications in the Education Economy: Towards the Performative Society? *Australian Educational Researcher,* 27(2): 1-23

Ball, S. J. (2003) The teacher's soul and the terrors of performativity. *Journal of Education Policy* 18(2): 215-228.

Beach, D. (2004) Labs and the quality of learning in school science: Schools, Labs and creativity, in Troman, G., Jeffrey, R. and Walford, G. (eds) *Identity, Agency and Social Institutions: Studies in Educational Ethnography Vol 10,* Oxford, Jai Press-Elsevier.

Borgnakke, K. (ed.) (2004) Et analytisk blik på senmodernitetens *gymnasium (*An analytic view on The Gymnasium in late modernity). *Gymnasiepædagogik 47, DIG, The University of Southern Denmark.*

Craft, A., Jeffrey, B. and Leibling, M. (2001), *Creativity in Education,* London: Continuum.

Dovemark, M. (2004a) Pupil Responsibility in the Context of School Changes in Sweden: market constraints on state policies for a creative education, *European Educational Research Journal*, 3(3): 658-673.

Dovemark, M. (2004b) Ansvar-flexibilitet-valfrihet. En etnografisk studie om en skola I förändring (Responsibility-flexibility-freedom of choice: An ethnographic Study of a School in Transition), Göteborg: *ACTA Universitatis Gothoburgensis* nr. 223.

Dovemark, M. and Beach, D. (2004) New aims and old problems in Swedish schools: flexibility, freedom of choice and self-reliance in learning as part of social reproduction, in Troman, G. Jeffrey B. and Walford, G. (eds) (2004) *Identity, Agency and Social Institutions in Educational Ethnography. Studies in Educational Ethnography*, 10: 123-140. Oxford: Jai Press.

Lyotard, J. F. (1979) *The Postmodern Condition: A report on knowledge*, Manchester: Manchester University Press

Seltzer, K., and Bentley, T. (1999) *The creative age*, London: Demos.

Pollard, A. Triggs, P, with Broadfoot, P. McNess, E., and Osborn, M. (2000) W*hat pupils say: changing policy and practice in primary education,* London: Continuum

Raggl, A., and Shratz, M. (in Press) Using visuals to release pupil voice: Emotional pathways to enhance thinking and reflecting on learning in Pole, C. (ed.) Seeing is Believing? Approaches to Visual Research Studies in *Qualitative Methodology,* 7.

Sugrue, C. (2004) Structure and Agency in the Construction of Creative Teaching and Learning: A View from the Margins, paper presented in the Ethnography in Education Group, *ECER,* Crete, September.

Troman, G. Jeffrey, B. (2006) Providing a framework for a 'shared repertoire' in a cross-national research project, in Walford, G. Troman, G. Jeffrey, B., *Methodological issues and practices in ethnography:, Studies in Educational Ethnography*, 11: 207-226.

Whitty, G. Edwards, T. (1998) School policy choices in England and the United States: an exploration of their origins and significance. *Comparative Education* 34: 211-227.

Woods, P (1993) *Critical Events in Teaching and Learning,* London. Falmer Press.

Woods, P. (1996) *Researching the art of teaching: ethnography for educational use,* London: Routledge.

Yeatman, A. (1994) *PostPostmodern revisionings of the political*, New York: Routledge.

Creative learning in an infant school

Félix Angulo Rasco; José Betanzo Sánchez; Ángeles Córdoba Arana;
Eulalia García Cruz; Eulogio García Vallinas; Mónica López Gil; José Ojeda
Díaz; Ramón Porras Vallejo, (Coord.); Carmen Pilar Rodríguez González;
Raquel Rodríguez Romero; Rosa Vázquez Recio and Rocí Villanego Chaza
Lace group, University of Cadiz

Introduction

In this chapter we aim to explain the main features that describe creative learning, based on the research carried out by one of the three cases framed in the CLASP Project, situated at an infant school. The pedagogical concepts of the teaching team are the basis for creative learning and for the organisation and management of the centre and their local adaptations of the municipal authority's educational policies.

These concepts derive overtly from authors such as Piaget, Luria and Stamback, but there are also a series of implicit theories employed emanating from Dewey, Kilpatrick, Vygotsky and Freinet. From the first author we can extract the importance of starting from real experience, from life, from the proximity, so that we can achieve real learning (Dewey, 1897, 1916). Kilpatrick (1921) argues in favour of projects as a means of giving a sense of scholarly work and to keep the students motivated. From Vygotsky we see the importance of interacting among equals and social cooperation for development (Vygotsky, 1979), together with the use of language as a tool of thinking (Vygotsky, 1977). The use of the assembly as a starting point for the daily activity, along with the 'natural' way of considering academic learning, is redolent of Celestin Freinet (1968, 1969).

Although our approach has been based on the description of creative learning from the student's perspective (Jeffrey, 2001), previous works describing creative teachers, along with teaching environment and skills promoting creative learning have been very useful (Woods, 1993, 1995).

Research context

Cigarrón is one of the two municipal infant schools in Puerto Real (Cádiz). The town is medium sized (about 40,000 inhabitants). The school building consists of two houses, with a large garden, connected by a long, light corridor fitted out for very young children. The school caters for groups of children of different ages (between one and five-years-old). There is one class for one-year-old children, two for two-year-old, one for four-year-old and one for five-year-old. There is not any group for three-year-old children because of administrative changes, although up to now there has always been one. The total number of children is eighty-eight, with five teachers and three assistants. The school is run by the Council. It is not free, but a sliding scale for the monthly fees has been established, depending on the families' incomes.

The teaching team considers children up to five-years-old as one complete educational stage and not as two cycles (0-3/3-6). To achieve this, they have always tried to ensure that the teacher working with the one year-old group continues with them until they reach the age of five.

The educational team has developed, for about thirteen years, an educational plan of its own, peculiar to the school, based on various educational aims and theoretical concepts of learning and development, fruits of the work and the reflections of the teachers who fundamentally defend infant education as a global, continuous educational stage up to six-years-old. This consideration constitutes the pedagogic reference in the daily work of the teachers. The curriculum is adapted to the necessities detected by the educational team, in a process of reflection and educational analysis of any situation, space, material, personal interaction, etc. that happens in the school. In the pattern of infant education developed in this school, it is up to the school to select and to organise aspects of the daily reality.

Their own evolutionary development approach consists of an indispensable sequence of activities. The success of this approach depends upon the teacher's understanding of the children, to know each boy and girl's evolutionary moment, towards where he/she goes, and therefore, what interpretation he/she makes of the world and what learning he/she can carry out.

The students are the central focus and the school activities are chosen according to the interests of the children. Teachers and pupils give importance to communication and language, to socio-affective factors and to interpersonal relationships. In addition, the relationships between the families and the school are very close, so much so that the parents participate in everything that happens in the school, this year spending every Wednesday morning in the school experiencing and participating in the activities. Significant learning is promoted in the educative process, with meaningful activities for children.

The classroom doors are always open and all internal spaces—kitchen, toilets, corridors are used by all the members of the school community and are exploited in the teaching/learning process. The children are autonomous: they know all the internal spaces in the school, can make suggestions, can take decisions, and know where to find every storybook and toy.

The teachers work in a team, they discuss the proposals, take decisions, talk about the children and share situations. And in order to do this, the teachers have agreed to meet at various times: in the morning, after the children have left, one afternoon a week and any time in the morning when they can talk about their work.

The assembly: student decision-making about what and how they learn, control of the activity

Each session usually starts, except in exceptional circumstances, with a class assembly. There is a space next to the entrance door, where the children put out their own chairs, gradually making an oval. The children and the teacher put their chairs on the same side of the classroom and nobody has a fixed place.

The assembly is where the children discuss, negotiate, agree, define and decide what they are going to do in each session. The curriculum is created and recreated day after day via the assembly process, with a great deal of student involvement.

> The teacher asked, 'What do you want to do today? What do you want to play?' They make suggestions, the first, 'the blind hen'. Accidentally the teacher says 'the white hen'. They all laugh and someone says 'the white hen'. The teacher says that if they want to, they can invent the game between themselves. Then they start to suggest 'new' games or games that others don't know and they explain them.   (Observation 11 April 2003).

But the assembly does not only deal with ideas or the suggested activities, but also the attitudes, desires, values, conflicts, relationships between equals and with adults. The assembly is something serious and important for everyone, because what is agreed there will carry an individual obligation and, at the same time, a collective one. As a result, gradually, over time, various rules have been introduced which evolve according to new situations and needs that arise. Some examples are:

- ◆ they must put any game or material that they have in their hands in the centre of the oval, on the floor, so that they can pay attention better.
- ◆ they can speak one at a time, after putting up their hand and waiting their

turn, which is usually regulated by the teacher.

•   they have to listen to the person talking.

•   first, everyone can make their suggestions and if someone makes one, they must explain it to the rest.

•   when there are no more suggestions they vote on them one by one, with each person only able to vote once for one of the suggestions.

In the assembly, they decide on activities or projects that could last from one day up to two or three weeks and discuss the demands imposed by the activity, both in terms of processes and results. They also take into account the individuality and autonomy of each child. So, when deemed necessary, the teacher reminds them of the continuing obligation to undertake the task or function upon which they previously decided.

> At the end of the morning they read a story that had been voted for in the assembly. They don't like it because it doesn't have pictures. The teacher says, 'What did you vote for this morning? To read the story. And what did I say to you? Look, it doesn't have pictures ... And then what did you say?' A child answers, 'We said it didn't matter because it was about dead people'. The teacher answered, 'As we've voted for it, we have to read it, don't we? Those that don't like it can do something else, can't they?' (Observation 20 March 2003)

An unwillingness to impose or force the children to do anything is appreciated. All the activities start from their desire, interest, fun, enjoyment, free acceptance without losing respect for diversity, different ways of knowing, thinking, feeling, expressing oneself, making relationships, communicating.

> While everyone goes to watch the film, I prefer to work on the dolls dress.
> (Observation 9 May 2003)

It is very important that each child can be him or herself, leaving their identities fluid. During the wedding project, for example, the first activity that they decided to carry out was to design their own party outfits. To do this, each one drew the outfit they would like to wear to the wedding, taking into account, of course, and the role that they would play, i.e. if they were the groom, bride, guest or judge. In the drawing they had to identify the pieces of the outfit and the accessories they would have to make later. Each child decided freely how they wanted to dress for the occasion and the resulting designs were very diverse. They captured their identities in the drawings and later in the outfits. The children knew they had to stick to their original drawings, so from then on they had to recreate the ideas represented on paper as closely as possible.

It can be seen that the student is usually the one that plans and chooses the moment and the way of playing games and doing activities. The teacher intervenes to motivate, help when necessary and assess the activity along with the children. The children participate in decision-making concerning the selection of activities and the organisation of the space and time to carry them out. The children also usually decide with which classmates they want to work. In this way, three groups were established: the giraffes, the tigers and the clowns. The children mixed freely and changed groups frequently depending on their interest in the type of activity or their affinity with classmates. They can also even decide to go to another class for part of a session because it is doing something that interested them.

> In the foam room the older and younger children are playing at hitting each other with some cushions. 'There's a problem' says the teacher 'One moment! The little ones are crying because they don't want to play rough and you'—aimed at the older ones—'hit them hard. How can we sort it out?' One of the older boys answers, 'Well, we'll make two parts (in the classroom): one to play at fighting and the other to play something else.'
>
> (Observation 27 March 2003)

The projects: the relevance and meaning of what is learnt

An essential element of the education and curricula of the centre projects is the principle of starting from the experiences, events, conflicts, interests and needs of the children themselves. It brings real life into the classroom and takes the classroom out into the real world:

> A father and mother who were interviewed talking about their daughter. 'It can't be said ... that she comes out of school and forgets it. If she has a problem here at school, she takes it there [home]. If she has a problem at home, she brings it here'. (Interview, 30 March 2003).

Various excursions were undertaken, such as the visit to the school where the majority will go in the next academic year, a visit to a shopping centre to buy food for a project, an excursion to the Algaida pine forest, and they have participated in local events such as a demonstration against the Iraq war. These activities developed in their class sessions with the teachers arguing that they are educational.

> The children had written a letter to parents saying that they were thinking of making a lemon mousse and asking how much a carton of cream, a lemon and a tin of condensed milk would cost. They read the replies the parents gave them and arrived at the conclusion that it would cost 4 euros or so. The teacher asked them to think how they could get the money and to make suggestions to the group.
>
> (Observation 13 March 2003)

After the excursion, they made a drawing of the route from the centre to the supermarket and they made the lemon mousse.

Everyone's life is an important subject to talk about in the school. This happens in various situations, such as in the assembly, with parents when the children are arriving and leaving the centre, in teacher interviews with families or during the day long parental visit to the classroom.

> Last year we introduced the door thing. It was our idea: arriving and leaving, to speak to each one that was also good for us. And this year we are going a step further and we have started parent visits to the centre, which have worked well up to now and have been useful to us ...
>
> (Teacher interview, 28 May 2003)

The teachers always seem to be alert to the possibility of an interesting topic arising that could generate rich learning-teaching experiences and/or socio-affective development. On some occasions, the project being worked on causes students to make comments about their experiences at home with their family. When this happens the teacher does not think twice about stopping the activity for a moment and discussing the subject openly in the assembly.

> Today in assembly they were talking about how they are going to organise themselves to prepare the wedding. Then A. asked to speak and said that

her parents were separated. She mentioned an incident at home with her mother. The teacher immediately left aside the wedding preparations, in order to clarify A.'s feelings. I had the impression that all the other students were clear about the fact that they were talking in order to make A. feel better. (Observation 6 May 2003)

For the teachers, these situations constitute a very important part of the curriculum: the socio-affective area. And they are always very alert to the moment in which socio-affective aspects arise, this being an important aspect to emphasise when considering the educational concept that the school tries to create and promote.

We have almost given more importance to the socio-affective than the conceptual ... perhaps because without a solid and stable socio-affective base. It's very difficult to achieve the cognitive. (Teacher interview, 25 June 2003)

The particular family situation of each child is very much taken into account: the separation of the parents, the birth of a baby brother or sister, an important date in their lives, worries or unhappiness shown by a child. For example, both parents and pupils displayed certain concerns about the change of school that was approaching for the next academic year. The teaching team planned to visit it.

They have visited the school to which the majority of children will go in the next academic year. In yesterday's assembly they made suggestions about what they needed or wanted to ask the pupils, the teachers or the director of the school. They suggested asking, 'Do you have assemblies?' 'Do you count up to 100?' (Observation 20 May 2003)

It is a conscious task to integrate all these realities and needs into the daily practice and use them to bring about highly significant learning. It seems that the children have entered a work dynamic that allows them to talk to their classmates about their feelings, ideas and concerns; they give the impression that they know that both their teacher and their classmates will listen to them and take them seriously.

Rather than starting with an academically designed and fixed curriculum, the teacher starts from the everyday life that surrounds her pupils, and adopts an individual basis, when constructing the curriculum:

> *Mother*: …What I tell her about my daughter, she (the teacher) knows much more.   (Interview with a mother, 30 April 2003.)

Some of the activities and projects that we have experienced in our time doing observations, that yielded certain information, were the following:

+ the **school garden,** shared by the whole school. It is a very large project that consists of various activities: they study the sowing times of different vegetables, how to look after, maintain and harvest them, they investigate different ways of cooking the different products they obtain.

+ the **lemon mousse** project that, as we have previously mentioned, consisted of the making of this dessert. To do this, they made handicrafts to sell to parents in a market. Once they had obtained the money, they made a list of ingredients they had to buy. Then, they did some drawings with which to explain the project to their parents and they asked them for permission to go to the supermarket to buy the ingredients. They went to the supermarket and bought what they needed, and drew pictures of the route they had taken from the centre to the supermarket. Finally, they made the mousse and ate it together.

+ the **wedding.** They had money left over from the lemon mousse project, so they decided to organise a wedding and buy sweets with this money for the reception. The wedding involved various activities: making outfits, decorations, asking parents to bring drinks, preparing the ceremony, making the invitations and having the wedding.

+ the **films** they watch. Generally, on Fridays they watch films that the children bring from home. But before and after showing them they talk about the story, the characters and the ideas that come out of the film. They also do drawings of scenes from the films.

> The assembly starts. Yesterday they decided that today there would be a film (there is one almost every Friday). They have brought various films from home. They talk about them. They vote to see 'Porky'.
> (Observation 9 May 2003)

In the same way, other activities, such as the songs they sing and dance to, the excursions, the rain game, seem like a game to them; a fun, exciting adventure in which more purely academic learning takes on a practical meaning: communicating via speech, drawing and writing, 'reading' messages, making advertising posters, calculating quantities, adding up, taking away. In the middle of an activity that could at times seem chaotic, in which different groups or individuals undertake different tasks not always directly related to the project, there is a sense of enthusiasm in the work atmosphere in which everyone is aware that they are doing something important and meaningful.

> They allocate roles e.g. prepare the room, make the tickets—for this there are two girls—they make tickets and put on the time and the picture of the film, they make posters to advertise the film.
> (Observation 9 May 2003)

There is evidence of the awareness of the consequences of team work, of defining tasks, of carrying them out to allow other classmates to do their work.

> The children control themselves: 'You have played with it and now you don't want to put it away, do you?' says a child to two others.
> (Observation 22 April 2003).

It is clear that the children are aware of the learning process and normally this is manifested in their self-control and in the importance they place on the tasks and functions to be carried out.

The autonomy of pupils in an inclusive school: the feeling of what belongs to them; it is their school, class, game.

Children's autonomy develops through development of the feeling that everything belongs to them: their school, their class and their games. The children are very clear that the activities, the classroom, materials, the spaces although shared, are theirs. As a project goes on, the teacher feels the need to remind the children of outstanding duties and tasks still needing completion by some children, but in general tasks depend on the autonomy and responsibility of the pupils.

They have organised the festival. All the tasks have been allocated. The teacher asked, 'What was the clown group going to do?' The children answer, 'Sell the bar tickets.' 'And the lion group, what were they going to do?' They answer, 'take the toys to the tin can game.' 'Good, but remember that we have to organise ourselves to carry the tables and chairs altogether.'

(Observation 4 June 2003)

This usually happens both when the tasks are fun as well as when they are more routine or require greater effort—such as preparing the classroom, each morning, putting the chairs down. In addition, the teacher tries not to force the situation, giving each child a margin of decision or giving the task an element of play.

In the patio they go to collect up the cars and bicycles they have used during break. They act out a car park. The teacher says, 'Let's see your car, sir.' The children answer, 'Here you are', making the gesture of paying. She says, 'Here's your ticket' (giving them a piece of scrap paper). Afterwards she congratulates them on the speed and efficiency they showed in putting everything away.

(Observation 25 April 2003)

They like to play the main role, have autonomy, be able to decide, participate. They want to be relied on, they want their opinion (individual and collective) on anything they are going to do to be considered. This seems to make them feel more proud of their work, the things they produce and their exchanges and transactions.

The four-year-olds are angry with a teacher who had asked them for some drawings and work some time ago saying that she would give them back and had not done so yet. She explained to them that she needed the items for a piece of work with other teachers, who needed to see how they worked. The children didn't agree and suggested that she photocopy the work and give them back the originals, because they wanted to take them home with the rest of their work.   (Observation 18 June 2003)

Normally the children have a wide margin of decision-making when deciding what and how to do something. Once they have chosen one of the suggestions from the class assembly, which may have been from their own initiative, from a classmate or from another teacher, they look for a personal way to carry it out.

> Today there is no assembly. Yesterday they decided they were going to see the film *The Little Whale*. Now they want to dance. Some girls and a boy dance ... They use plastic ice creams as microphones and sing while they dance. Some that don't want to dance are the band or the audience. They use pieces of plastic as trumpets and play the music.
> (Observation 30 May 2003).

They seem constantly engaged in defending their own identities and trying to reflect them in their language, movements, drawings and play. They watch each other and have an open attitude to what is new or to what is an alternative way to do things. Learning involves extensive oral language: they ask, inform, discuss, suggest and explain.

> Two girls make the tickets. They work together. One, who is better at writing, directs the task. The other puts the price on the back, while the first writes TICKET and does a small drawing. The one writing the price is tired and starts doodling on her part. The other girl looks at the pile they have done (more than 30) and says, 'Some are bad'. The other says, 'Of course, they're for the little children ... they don't understand, so it doesn't matter'. (Observation 9 May 2003)

The teachers create a climate of confidence, camaraderie, mutual support, respect and tolerance of diversity or different choices, nor if it was boring, monotonous, or repetitive. They try to work with respect for difference, for the different ways of understanding, thinking, feeling, expressing oneself, making relationships, communicating. They value the idea that each child can be him or herself.

Each child is allowed to find his or her way of doing things, making connections with his or her experiences and life, as can be seen from the following fragment.

> They discussed how to get the money to make the lemon mousse. One of the children suggested, 'What about if we get a newspaper and cut the paper into the shape of money?' The teacher said to him and everyone

else, 'Yes? Do you think that's OK? What do you all think?' Another
girl answered, 'No, they aren't going to want us to pay them with fake
money. We have to do something else.' The teacher said, 'Well, come on,
let's think of something else ...'   (Observation 13 March 2003).

As the activity was planned and started, the teacher invited the children to
make contributions, ideas and perspectives or to suggest changes and variations
that, normally, serve to enrich and differentiate the tasks according to the diversity
in the classroom, such as this example that occurred whilst they were playing
the rain game.

A boy makes a very original umbrella using five pieces of plastic.
The rest imitate him ... A girl has turned an umbrella upside down
(with the strips of plastic up instead of down), because 'it has been
taken by the wind'. They start to imitate the sound of the wind ...
                              (Observation 22 April 2003)

No child gets the impression that they are mistaken or they have done
something wrong. Here is palpable reality, you 'learn by your mistakes'.
There is also a type of *serendipity*. The things that arise as variations during
a piece of work, are explained and integrated into the activity, which, although
relatively simple and uniform at the beginning, gradually take on more nuances
and derivations, becoming, at the end of the process, a product enriched with the
contributions of all the children, a product that in some way belongs to them.
Various ways of achieving the participation of all pupils and the consequent
enrichment of the process can be identified:

+ during games, via the encouragement of options and the different ways of
developing them as in the following case:

playing, a boy lies down in a house, (improvised under some tables), next
to a girl (his sister) and she asks him, 'Are you a dog?' He says, 'No'. She
replies, 'Then you can't sleep here'. He answers, 'Why not? men and dogs
can sleep here ...'   (Observation 22 April 2003)

+ discussing, questioning, asking for explanations in the assemblies, of other
children and teachers of other classes;
+ asking for explanations of paper and pencil work (drawings, etc.);

+ suggesting media and resources, real or imaginary, with which to play or work;
+ not accepting suggestions 'as is': having to justify them and rationalise them;
+ provoking participation: 'let's see, let's think.'

Autonomy in carrying out activities also extends to autonomy in the resolution of interpersonal conflicts, which are also part of the school's agenda. It seems that the teachers stress the importance of children learning to resolve their conflicts and problems between themselves. They try to give them basic ideas and very clear rules for problem-solving. Amongst these rules two seem to be stressed as very important: one, respect for the wishes of the other and two, the defence of ones own wishes and interests, not allowing them to be manipulated by others.

> Two girls get angry with the teacher and complain, 'You always tell us to sort it out ourselves ...', asking for her intervention.
> (Observation 29 April 2003)

Parents are also aware of these demands for autonomy in conflict resolution:

> *Father*: 'The day I was there, something caught my attention, at one moment in the class I remember that a kid went to the teacher and said, 'So and so is hitting me', and she replied, 'Speak to her and sort it out'. She didn't say 'I'll go with you, what's happened? What have you done, tell her to come here, stay here' That is to say, if you have had a fight with him, go and sort it out.'
> (Interview 30 April 2003)

Collaboration and participation: the sense of community, the 'open door' policy

The 'open door' principle partly forces the maintenance of joint responsibility between the teachers, given that although each teacher has her classroom and her list of children, in practice it works as if all the children were with all the teachers.

Here, although you have a space in which you are with your group, your children, it's not the organisation of your classroom that is important, it's the organisation of the centre, understand?

(Interview, 28 May 2003)

This demands rich and wide communication channels between teachers, something which they spend time on every morning and every Wednesday afternoon. In addition, they have to agree on the allocation of responsibilities, the rules to negotiate and uphold with the participation of the pupils, the use of common spaces.

The pupils, the older ones (4 and 5 years-old) in this case, also participate in this community spirit, and are a clear help in looking after and teaching the younger ones. They are often working with something dangerous and if a very young child goes into the class of 4 year-olds the alarm is sounded straightaway. 'Be careful, a little one!' And the dangerous materials are put away. The older children are normally told about the dangers of some materials and seem to be on the alert to avoid a very young child hurting themselves.

While they are eating the potato salad they have made, a teacher asks the older children to keep their eyes open 'in case they see a younger child pick up a fork and take it away from the table. Tell them that the fork is for eating potatoes.' Quickly an older girl checks on the forks that are around the plate from which she is eating potatoes.

(Observation 20 March 2003)

At a specific point in the morning, one classroom could be half-empty and the one next door quite full, because an interesting activity has arisen and the children have moved to the appropriate classroom.

At the end of the morning all the children who want to will go to see the film, but they have to have a ticket.

(Observation 9 May 2003)

In short, it can be seen that, although the children tend to stay in their classroom, at the slightest sign of something that interests them, they can change activity and move to another classroom or another part of the school.

The possibilities for collaboration, for mutual help, for co-involvement in tasks are present on a community level, on a school level and, of course, on a classroom level.

> We always say it. Don't face these things alone. We work in a team and say 'look with this child this happens', ... we take it on board, although only you see it, we take on board everybody's opinion. You check it out with your team, the team gives you ideas and probably something you haven't thought of comes up in the team. (This dynamic of staff team work) is in the very organisation of the school ...
>
> (Interview, 28 May 2003).

This principle seems to be an essential part of the educational project. In fact, the teachers meetings we attended and the interviews with teachers and parents promoted a teamwork dynamic which transmitted a model of co-operation which is easily taken on board by the children, who despite being so young tend to meet their classmates to collaborate over activities or to resolve conflicts or problems between themselves.

The circumstances and situations that facilitate collaboration are the following:

* the spaces, the tables, the corners, workshops (inside and outside the classroom) invite group work.
* the materials are communal and shared and are not very plentiful.
* time is used polychronically (various activities take place at the same time) and functional (it is at the service of ...) although there are moments when collaboration is more prone to happen: arriving in the morning—lunch—putting away—assembly. Most of the games imply collaboration: allocation of roles and tasks, discussion, planning, choice and allocation of materials.

> They are going to make potato salad with the potatoes they have collected from the garden. They are going to add hard-boiled eggs they have boiled and onions that the teachers have brought. They decide to share the work of peeling between everyone who wants to participate: everyone has a potato or an egg so they can collaborate. Some of them think its disgusting and prefer to bring the cutlery or the ingredients.
>
> (Observation 20 March 2003)

- the projects require the collaboration of the whole class. Normally individual and group responsibilities are assigned, but everyone knows it is a communal task. It is a group project, they share objectives, resources, dreams, difficulties and achievements. Mutual help is often generated.
- watching a film on a Friday, from its choice in assembly to the organisation and implementation of its showing, requires a great deal of joint action.

> For the film *Porky* that they wanted to see they agree on the picture for the poster: a little dog that is abandoned and goes to live with Porky. Those that finish the poster, explain on the board what is in the older children's corridor   (Observation 9 May 2003).

But collaboration also arises in resolving conflicts between themselves, as we have already mentioned, it can be seen that the teachers usually try to get children to solve their problems themselves, using dialogue and with the least possible intervention by teachers as well as when giving or receiving help in a game or task.

> A girl complains that a classmate, who is playing in a corner whilst the teacher is reading a story to other children, is making too much noise with some pieces of wood. The girl says to the teacher, 'It's just that he's making too much noise with the wood and I can't hear the story'. The teacher says, 'Well go and tell him. Tell him why he is bothering you and sort it out by talking to him.'   (Observation 20 March 2003)

Constructed and creative learning

The concept of learning that appears to prevail in the centre is one which starts from the interests and autonomy of the pupils and a respect for the learning needs which at any moment the children demonstrate.

> When you go into a classroom where they are working on a project you see that one is playing, the other is doing something else, the other is listening to music. In this apparent disorder there is an internal order and, when you stay in the classroom for a while, you see that the children have systematised what they are doing and

that everyone knows what they are doing and why they are doing it.'
(Interview, 25 June 2003).

This concept of learning seems to be reflected in the working methodology in the school: they watch each other, ideas are communicated and discussed, they have an open attitude to what is new and to new ways of doing things. When they decide what they are going to play, the first thing they have to do is explain the rules of the game, '*how do you play that?*' They try to develop, from the rules of other games or other experiences, a new way to play and have a good time. They rehearse their roles, invent new ones, they are alert to any variation that occurs to anyone in order to try it out or, on occasions, contribute their own way of developing it.

> They choose to play 'lions and tigers'. But now they have to explain how to play it. A girl corrects them, 'lions and lionesses'. The teacher says 'then tigers too?' 'No, tigresses', someone replies. Rather than explaining the game, they start to choose their roles: 'I want to be a tiger' 'I'm a lioness' 'I'm an animal keeper.' 'Where shall we play?' asks the teacher. After a discussion they decide to play in the 'foam'. 'And how do you play it?' 'They make their house, they eat, they sleep.'   (Observation 11 April)

Normally there is an attitude of constant searching: they look at what others do, they ask them what and how they do things, give their opinion. They have a special 'receptor' to catch the suggestions made by the teacher.

> The teacher gives an idea: she takes two plastic ice creams and says that they are maracas. Then a child picks them up. Another child also wants them and starts to look around the classroom for two other objects that could serve the same purpose.'   (Observation 30 May 2003)

They observe their surroundings in order to find objects or places to use as a basis for something new. Their imagination takes off while they are active and, at the same time, they look for an explanation of this action. The dialogue between them is constant. Except in the assembly when they have to speak and listen according to their turn, the rest of the time the communication is fluid, rich, varied. They are continually asking about or explaining what they are doing, what happens, motives, reasons.

The teacher's constant intention is that the child should be aware of their learning:

> She has a way of capturing the roles of the children in specific moments, when they play in the kitchen, that you probably don't realise, they are playing, but she has knowledge about the subject, she's taking notice 'look what she's doing, look what he's doing ...' She's learning and knows where each child is going, what they mean, what they aspire to at this age, what they are looking for, what they are trying to do.
> (Interview pad3cig, page. 4. 21 May 2003)

The whole session or cycle of tasks, games, projects, culminates with the invitation, sometimes a demand, to each child to recount, draw, explain what he or she has done, why, what rules there are, what he or she has learned.

> *Girl:* 'What we do, we draw'.
> *Interviewer:* 'Why do you draw it?'
> *Girl:* 'We draw it because we want to, we draw what we do and that way we don't forget'   (Interview, June 2003)

It is possible that without this encouragement from the teacher, these usually active beings would not go so deeply into what they have learned. They make frequent evaluations about how much fun is enjoyed, how interesting it is, how important what they have learnt is. This type of process causes children to connect the activities implemented in school with other learning, compare them, situate them and 'carry' them to other contexts, like that of the family.

> When we are at home and maybe we are arguing and we don't agree with her and she says, 'You have to put up your hand', and therefore all that, clearly, allows you to maintain a conversation, first she speaks, then you speak and that way you can understand each other ... My daughter arrives with a recipe 'Mum, we have to make fried aubergines, because look, you cook aubergines like this...', at 5 years-old!
> (Interview, 21 May 2003)

It is not considered that creative learning is limited to one area of the curriculum, like music, dance or artistic or literary expression. It is much more than that. It is every learning process that has the characteristics of participation, ownership, control, relevance and innovation. Diversity in expressing feelings, ideas and using materials is valued and encouraged. They have different ways of using spoken and written language. They write using only the vowels of each word or strokes according to the syllables or *bits* of words if they are not using the vowels yet. With numbers they also use strokes according to the amounts if they do not yet know their numbers.

> You have to say when they bring you drawings home, to say 'What is she able to capture of that word?' The vowels, which I imagine are what children get first. So she came with a piece of writing with the vowels that she had caught of the word.
>
> (Interview, 21 May 2003)

> They are doing a worksheet containing groups of objects which they have to count and write the number. One child doesn't know how to write numbers and puts strokes.　　　　(Observation 29 April 2003)

Drawing (in small or big formats), movement, dance, music and songs, stories (more or less invented), handicrafts, costumes, games, and the unusual (imaginative) use of objects are also appropriate vehicles for creative learning.

All of these are ways of facilitating creative, original, personal learning by each child in the classroom. Of course it is clear that the main purpose of this way of teaching is to encourage a reflection of the way that each child has experienced each activity via a drawing, or assessing the work done. The children know how to do this already and many of them do not need to be encouraged to do it: they do it naturally. Others are reminded when they are attracted by something new and want to leave the previous work behind.

> The teacher concentrates on helping a child so that he can do a drawing, he had done a scribble and left it to one side. She guides him with questions about the people he wants to draw.　　　　(Observation 9 May 2003)

The most common way to do this is by drawing a picture of the event or activity. On this picture they usually write something, in addition to their name. But they also explain it with words, they narrate it, they incorporate it into some kind of record, although they are usually latent (during and after the activity), in which they answer questions such as: What have we learnt? How did we do it? Did we have a good time? What didn't work very well?

> They go back to class to draw the game in order to put it in the 'Games Book'. While they draw, the teacher speaks to them about the game and the connection between the drawing and what they have done.
>
> (Observation 11 April 2003)

Even so, perhaps the most enriching are the exchanges of ideas and opinions between the children themselves, as well as the evaluations they make of their own performance and participation and that of others, with regard to both cognitive and affective or relational aspects. The learning of respect for others, for the rules that they create and continually recreate (although some are more stable), for the non-violent and reasoned resolution of conflicts (frequently over the use of space or materials, or over the allocation of roles in games) is of great importance. And they take these matters very seriously. They give importance to the judgement or recommendations of the teacher, but also to those that come from their classmates and from themselves.

Conclusions

At the infant school under study, the students seem to be at the centre of their learning and to participate in fundamental aspects of this such as the organisation of tasks and the classroom and what, how, where and who to work with. They feel and take ownership of their knowledge and the process of constructing it. They control the time needed to undertake their work and/or their games. They assimilate different ways of working so that the format of the activities need not be the same for the whole group. They decide what materials they need to use and with whom they have to share them. All this is a way of contributing to constructive learning that is closely connected with what really interests and concerns those at the centre of it, the children.

References

Dewey, J. (1897) My Pedagogic Creed. *School Journal*, 54(3): 77-80.

Dewey, J. (1916) *Democracy and Education*, NewYork: MacMillan.

Freinet, C. (1968). *La méthode naturelle. L'apprentissage de la langue*, Neuchâtel:Delachaux et Niestlé.

Freinet, C. (1969) *Les invariants pédagogiques*, Neuchâtel: Delachaux et Niestlé.

Jeffrey, B. (2001) Primary pupils' perspectives and creative learning, *Encyclopaideia* (Italian journal) 9 (Spring): 133-152

Kilpatrick, N. H. (1921) *The Project Method,* New York: The Teachers College, Columbia University.

Vygotsky, L. V. (1977) *Pensamiento y lenguaje,* (Spanish Edition), Buenos Aires: La Pléyade.

Vygotsky, L. V. (1979) *El desarrollo de los procesos psicológicos superiores,* (Spanish Edition), Barcelona:Crítica.

Woods, P. (1993) *Critical events in teaching and learning,* London: Falmer Press

Woods, P. (1995) *Creative teachers in primary school,* Buckingham: Open University Press.

The Bridge School:
Creative learning as community learning

Andrea Raggl
University of Innsbruck

Introduction

This chapter is about one particular school, 'Bridge' Primary School. The school offers an inspiring place for its eighty learners and seven teachers. In the last ten years the school has changed from an 'ordinary' school to a 'creative' school. The developments of Bridge School demonstrate the range of possibilities open to a school in Austria to reorganise its teaching and learning. Most obvious to visitors is the creative use of space: the outdoor environment and the indoor architecture. The creative use of space is a result of combined efforts of the community of teachers, learners and parents. These alliances inside school and beyond the school gate made new ways of communicating and cooperating possible and necessary. The development was a democratic process, where learners, teachers and parents saw themselves as important participants. Peter Woods argues that

> In the learning community all are teachers and all are learners, members of the general community included. There is a holistic approach to knowledge, there is ownership of knowledge, progressive development and continuous renewal and shared democratic leadership.
> (Woods 1999)

The case study will show how community learning can 'maximise the resources of the school, to provide variety and novel experiences for the children' (Jeffrey and Woods 2003).

A learning school

Context

The main changes at Bridge school started ten years ago, when Richard T., started his career as a visionary head at this school. After decades of experience in progressive education as a teacher, with an emphasis on Freinet pedagogy he was keen to realise innovations beyond his own classroom which he could achieve as the head of a school. Changes were organised democratically as a result of his many years experiences of Freinet pedagogy. Freinet pedagogy symbolises a self-determinated pedagogy, an autonomy organised by the participants. It means primarily giving learning into the hands of children and offering them different possibilities for free expression, free speech and autonomous writing.

Richard T. retired in 2002, but the new head, Peter U. and the staff of the school continued the development of the school.

> Since I have been at this school, I really have to say, Richard (the head) has motivated and inspired me a lot to put even more effort into tackling the whole thing in a even more open-minded, freer manner. (Martina)

Martina had been an engaged teacher and had experienced child-centred pedagogy in small rural schools successfully before she came to Bridge School, 'I did not put myself under pressure, but the children learned their letters very easily ... that was no problem at all'.

The children inspired her teaching methods through books or through 'colleagues, whom I admired', she explains. However, when she came to Bridge School she found a creative field where she was encouraged to develop her full potential, supported by a visionary headmaster and a learning community which offered her a place to be a learner herself:

+   in regular staff meetings where the ongoing developments of the school are discussed;
+   with well equipped working places in the school;
+   with an excellent equipped library with journals and new media; and
+   with the 'workshop'—a room where teachers of the region can meet for exchanges and courses or to borrow books or journals.

These different aspects show that school itself is a 'learning school' (Schratz and Steiner-Löffler, 1999). Czikszentmihaly (1997) argues that only within a creative field where personal strengths are honoured can a creative person develop his or her full potential. Martina's story shows this distinctly. It is a reciprocal process. The context inspires her imagination and she adds her knowledge and ideas to the field, such as putting effort in building together with colleagues a clearly labelled storing system (boxes with materials for different topics). Instead of starting again from the very beginning, every teacher uses what's already there and also adds things to the different topics. Martina's competence in drama also contributes to the development of the school. She has completed further training in theatre pedagogy and since then she has placed an emphasis on theatre in the school and has built up a basic equipment of costumes, illumination techniques and microphones. Furthermore, she has inspired the community to create two excellent places for rehearsals and performances inside and outside the school. Seeing school as a stage enriches the learning culture by offering new forms of interactions and alternative experiences.

The developments at Bridge School were possible because of the democratic nature of the staff and beyond, as the former head, Richard T. wrote in his Ph.D.:

> You can discuss progressive education with parents and they are even willing to give financial support in order to create surroundings, which encourage a wide scope of experience in school. Parents are willing to work in the classrooms. They also appreciate it if their children learn to organise their work ... Change originates at the roots.

Here again the orientation towards Freinet pedagogy shows the development is coming from the base: it is a democratic process. Parents are involved 'institutionally' through the 'Society for the Sponsorship of the Bridge School', which was established in 1996. The major task of the society is

> ... to support the school in its development in such a manner as to enable the children to experience everyday school life as being more open to new ideas, more varied and eventful and more child-oriented.
> (Society's handout)

Members of the staff and members of the Society meet on a monthly basis in the school to discuss the ongoing developments, special events and fundraising together. Seeing parents as partners provides a 'strong political base' (Jeffrey and Woods 2003) as the following description of the development of the creative environment of the school shows.

The creative use of space

The creative environment emerged through the combined efforts of the school community. Teachers, parents and learners started to work in the school in their free time, organised events for raising funds, searched for sponsors. The commitment of parents made change possible on a large scale. The most obvious achievement was change through two projects: the 'forest project' and the 'library project'. Through the the parents' political influence, the school acquired a piece of land from the town, an undeveloped hill next to the school, to create an extensive forest playground. The other project was the creation of a suitably designed and well- equipped library.

The forest project

Places to climb and to hide, places to form gangs, to play games and to sit on benches, a space for playing and learning has emerged over the last eight years. In 2004, the forest project was completed and a container was purchased for the outdoor playing equipment. Children from all the classes transformed the brown container together with a local artist into a multi-coloured picture.

The first step was to remove an asphalt covering, a car park for the teachers of both the primary school and for the adjacent polytechnic. Negotiations with the local building authority and long discussions with teachers of the neighbouring polytechnic were necessary to realise the ideas of the primary school community.

Intensive discussions with the town's politicians were required to obtain the hill to create a forest playground and a 'forest arena'. Teachers and parents spent considerably amount of time together 'thinning' the forest and creating a diverse place to play and to learn. The area now offers a place where outdoor teaching activities can take place. There are theatre rehearsals and performances, music sessions and school celebrations for children, parents and friends of the school.

In 2003, the highlight of the school was installed, a big slide, which offers great fun for everyone throughout the year. The children now have a place at their disposal, which offers various possibilities in their school break, after school and in their spare time.

The library project

Apart from the creative use of the outdoor space, parents and teachers also worked on bringing about change inside the school building, the 'forum', an auditorium for meetings of all classes and rehearsals or performances and for the other main project, the library. The head of school used his connections with a teacher in a higher technical school who created a varied library landscape with plenty of book shelves, computer stations and with places to sit individually or in groups. Parents helped in finding sponsors for books.

Celebrating together

For several years now the community of the school has celebrated two big outdoor events, the spring and the autumn festivals. Apart from this, there are several smaller celebrations throughout the year. Learners and teachers prepare together drama, songs or dances for an audience of children, teachers, parents and friends of the school. Parents help with food and drinks. These celebrations offer the opportunity to get to know each other better, as one teacher describes:

> Closer relationships have developed because of the celebrations. For example, I always liked celebrating with children—organising celebrations *with* them, I mean. I have always been a bit cautious, as far as parents are concerned, because I have had a few negative experiences in this respect. Overall, however, when invited to take part, they become more relaxed and you can speak with them more easily.   (Martina)

It became obvious that taking part in working activities and celebrations offered possibilities for all participants to get to know each other, a basis for mutual understanding.

Cooperation beyond the classroom

The staff continually looked for possibilities to cooperate beyond the school to develop the context for learning. Teachers plan school wide projects together, such as the reading project, where pupils have the opportunity to explore books from the library in an unusual way. Different books were exhibited in the entrance hall once a week, each is marked with a colour associated with a school room. The children take the strip of colour of the chosen book with them and after the main school break time they go to the indicated rooms. As well as exploring books, this weekly event offers the oppurtunity to make contact with pupils and teachers of other classes. The school year is punctuated by special project days or project weeks, like a reading week at the beginning of April where the classrooms are broken up. The different forms of cooperation on an institutional level provide varied forms of cooperation for children as well. This has an impact on the social structures of a school, as the following example shows.

Learners as teachers—cooperation with children of different ages

Once a week learners of two classes, second and third form, work together for two hours on a same topic. Maria, an eight-year-old girl, from the third form, explains:

> What I like is that I can play a lot of things with Barbara (girl from Year 2). For example, if I'm working with my girlfriend and Barbara then there are three of us and then we can play *Memory* much better than if there were only the two of us.

Maria is one of the older learners who has taken over the role as a 'godparent'. They experience being responsible for younger ones, they are now the more capable peers (cf. Vygotsky 1978, p. 86) and act as teachers in the heterogeneous age group. Taking on a teaching role gives children control and an opportunity to be creative. Learners experience their own competencies by explaining something to somebody. In doing so they are also 'developing their understanding of the teaching and learning process' (Jeffrey and Woods 2003, p. 115). This includes, 'She gets on my nerves, she does not do what she should do!', as Sarah underlines. The eight-year-old girl obtains insights into teachers work such as persuading a pupil to do something, in which they are not interested. Sarah has to use her imagination to get her younger partner to do the given tasks. Learners also experience learning issues.

> It is not so fine because we can't get on as quickly as before—we used to finish the tasks in no time at all. Now we have to wait for the others until they have finished it, too.

Maria and her classmates have to learn to be patient with the younger learners. By doing this, students can experience differences and gain competencies in handling them. This collaboration has an impact on the social structure of the school, as the following dialogue with Maria and Doris indicates:

Interviewer: Why is it not fine, being small?
Doris: Because everybody makes fun of you.
Interviewer: Who makes fun of you?

Doris: When we were in the first class, the children in the second class always said, 'First class children need a baby's bottle!" (Doris and Maria in unison).

Interviewer: Do you say such things to the first class pupils, now? (both children shake their heads) No? Why not?

Maria: Because we are their 'godparents.'

The two girls indicate how the collaboration beyond the classroom borders influenced the community of learners in a school. If you have worked together with someone, you got to know her or him, you feel responsible for the person and this has an impact on the daily interactions—beyond adults control—such as in the school grounds or on the way to or from school.

Creative teaching promotes creative learning

Creative learning can not be taught but teachers can set the conditions by offering a fairly flexible framework for learners where children can come 'to own their own knowledge and skills, being enthused and changed by the process and having some control of the learning process, but under teacher guidance' (Jeffrey and Woods 2003). This enables children to build up the competencies which are needed to carry out tasks step by step and to take over more and more responsibility for the own learning. This is possible because the teacher starts by using children's 'prior knowledge'. This requires special skills, as Martina indicates.

If you observe learners, you know what's going on. And if you are not sure, you ask the child, and normally children are willing to tell you what's going on in their mind.

Observing children, asking them and listen to their narratives enables the teacher to understand them more and to offer the help the individual child's needs, without giving too little or too much. Setting the conditions for creative learning includes placing high value on the personal development of children.

You really have to take children as they are. Of course I want all my learners to be excellent writers. But if one learner is not such an excellent writer, I have to accept this as well. And if he is not such an excellent writer he will have other abilities—so the main thing is that he is managing his life. If I only look at his faults I would not help him at all.   (Martina)

The teacher shows she is looking beyond school. She looks at the individual resources of a child and tries to include them in the learning process. She is remodelling the learning process by responding to the interests and needs of her twenty-six pupils. As well as observating and speaking to learners individually, Martina is able to hear learners' voices in the assemblies which take place regularly.

In the assembly, learners can say everything. They tell me their interests, but they also tell me which tasks are not interesting at all.

Assemblies are a central aspect of Freinet pedagogy. It is lived democracy, 'Assemblies also offer them an opportunity to experience that they have different opinions', (Martina). The circle indicates every member of the assembly is equal. Everybody has the possibility to speak; everybody has to listen if someone else is speaking. The participants of the assembly learn to cope with diversity.

'Some who don't say a word at the beginning start to tell me their interests after a while', Martina explains. Children learn by observing others and sometimes they start articulating their interests as well, such as Doris who had been a silent child in her first two years. Doris made the following suggestion in the assembly: 'Can't we make presentations like my older sister does?' The class discussed her idea and presentations became a part of the learning in this class. Beetlestone argues:

The task is easy if the context is more flexible and if schools consider their resource provision. Imagination brings delightful freshness and originality of approach to enliven learning for both teachers and children.
(Beetlestone 1998)

The example of Diana shows that time is an important factor. If the framework is flexible, enough it enables all learners to contribute to the community. The teacher is able to act and react patiently because she feels in control: 'The curriculum is very open, if you read it the right way'. This knowledge enables her to reach the diverse range of needs the learners. Martina sees her main role in delivering the curriculum in a child-oriented way: 'Everything which has to do with nature, animals, and art, the children are really interested in'. With this child-orientation, she makes the curriculum more relevant to learners. The imaginative modification of the curriculum is possible because she knows it is up to her to decide, 'I would not be a teacher if somebody told me what to do'. Martina is in control of the methods and the topics and reacts flexibly to the interests and needs of the learners.

The learning experience itself

Learning at 'Bridge' derives from social constructivist principles. Together with their teachers and peers, learners interpret and reconstruct the experiences in a social context (cf. Jeffrey and Woods 2003).

Illustrations from the classroom

One task of the weekly plan is to learn a poem.

> The learners can choose one of three offered poems. Sarah, a seven-year-old girl, has a look at all of them. She shakes her head and asks her teacher, 'I don't like these poems. Can I look for another one?' The teacher looks at her, smiles and answers, 'For sure. Do you know where to look for it?' Sarah answers, 'Yes.' It does not take long and she finds a poem. She sits at her place and learns it. A bit later, the class assembles on the big carpet. The teacher asks the children, 'Who has learnt a poem today?' Some hands go up. 'And who wants to recite it?' A few of them want to do it. The teacher encourages one insecure boy to recite it together with his friend. Then she tells her pupils: 'And now we have got a different poem. Sarah decided to choose another one. Do you want to recite it, Sarah?' Sarah is very proud and she recites the long poem very well.
>
> (Field Note)

In illustration two

> Three girls are sitting at the computer. Next to them is a book about horses. They were looking for it in the library and are now working with it. 'We want to create our own horse book. We just started,' Maria answered when I asked her what they are doing. A classmate came towards them; they cover the monitor and shout, 'Don't look at it! It's a surprise! We will show it to you in the assembly when it's ready!' The classmate gets

even more interested in what they are doing because they are making a secret out of it but she leaves them and the girls continue their work with great concentration. A bit later, I'm at the other end of the aisle when one of them runs to me and asks, 'Can you help us? We can't find a button!' I follow her. The others are still trying to find the button for the quotation mark. After I've showed it to them one girl says, 'We have to go on now!'   (Field Note)

In illustration three we see how they establish control.

The lesson just started. The learners are sitting at their tables and wait for the teacher who is doing some organisational work. Maria is concentrating on her writing. It looks as though she does not hear or see much of what is happening around her. The teacher is telling the learners, 'You can start with your plan work now.' The learners start working on a self-chosen task of the weekly plan. Maria keeps on writing. I take the seat next to her, Maria looks up and shows me the stickers in front of her. Then she shows me her story she is writing and I ask her, 'Do you like writing stories?' Maria answers smiling, 'Yes, but only if I can decide what to write'   (Field Note)

Characteristics of creative learning

These illustrations show all learners working on a task they have chosen or at least have modified themselves. They are going beyond the given tasks. Bringing in their own interests they make learning more meaningful to them and by doing this they create something new, a new story, a new book, or a modified learning situation. Furthermore, they are in control of the learning process.

For example, Sarah fulfils the official tasks in her own way. She feels confident to criticise the tasks given by her teacher and asked if she could find a self-chosen poem. In the second illustration the three eight year-old girls use their time, after finishing the compulsory tasks, to work on a topic they are interested in, horses. The three of them are enthusiastic riders. They were working on their own with the help of a specialised book to create their own horse book. If support was needed they asked for it, in this case the researcher. Otherwise, they clearly indicated that they preferred doing the things on their own. Maria decided to write a story before the official lesson started. She likes writing stories—'but only if I can decide what to write', she emphasised. She works with concentration, showing a 'peaceful' face. She continued writing when the situation around her changed until she finished her story. Then she started to work on the given tasks like her classmates, only some minutes later.

All learners engage when they are active participants. One of the most obvious factors is that learners are absorbed in their activities for a considerable period of time. Beetlestone underlines, 'Children who are interested concentrate; if they see the relevance of the activity they will engage in it until they feel they have mastered it' (Beetlestone 1998). Engaged working also appears with common tasks, as the following example shows:

> Kathrin is concentrating on a maths task. When she was asked about her work, she explained: 'It's only me, who has it like this!' It is a common maths task, but instead of being given the numbers Kathrin has to roll the dice to get the numbers to solve the task. With dicing she gets unique numbers which makes the task a more personal one: 'It's *my* number', Kathrin stresses. Her numbers and her results are different to others.
>
> (Field note)

Learners as active and engaged participants act as co-creators of the learning situation. Learners contribute to the learning process with their ideas and they improve the quality of lessons with their suggestions making learning more relevant for them. Learners and teachers are creating a co-participative climate for learning (Jeffrey and Woods 2003).

The school as a stage: creative learning and theatre

'And most of all, I like drama', eight-year-old Sonja says while we were speaking about her favourite things at school. Sonja is attending the theatre course at school with eighteen other children (third and fourth forms) every second week in the afternoon. Her class teacher Martina is organising the course. Sonja and half of her classmates join in this activity. Drama plays an important role in everyday learning in Martina's class too. It is in accordance with the holistic approach of her pedagogy. The pupils practice short plays on their own or with the help of the teacher as part of the weekly plan. Pupils learn the art of acting across subject borders: they learn to read and practice plays; to rearrange them; to make up their own dialogues in the German lesson; to practice songs for the play in the Music lesson; to work for the stage design during the Drawing lesson and to work on movement and physical expression in Physical Education.

Theatre is a co-production of pupils and teachers (cf. Lenzen 1990). New methods of interaction between the teacher and the pupils can emerge. The adult does not only take command over the children's performance—she is part of the play, she is an observer just like the pupils, she gets ideas from them, she needs their commitment. She appears as a narrator, helps with rebuilding the scene, accompanies the pupils as they sing with the piano or the guitar. They can encounter each other in different roles, more than just as teachers and learners. The various forms of interaction allow everyone to get to know each other in different situations. The play is a result of combined efforts—in this process personal strengths and weakness have to be admitted and can be used creatively (cf. Lenzen 1990). They all know that they depend upon each other and, with their collective aim of performing well, they stick together as a group.

The teacher takes ideas where she finds them—adapts them, even writes her own plays, if something is important to her. She did this within the framework of a reading project in spring 2004. Children in her class performed a play, which dealt with the problem as to why some children prefer sitting in front of the television to reading books. The teacher took an every-day topic of children's culture and offered them a productive explanation of it (cf. Lenzen 1990 p. 15). Children can play with their culture, can alienate it and see other layers of reality.

This creative process offers possibilities to experience alternative ways of acting and thinking. Children are motivated to learn their parts, even if it means extra work at home.

> I learn with my father the texts of the play … For example he is my partner there—the one I have to talk with and then it is much easier. He always says, 'Read a line' and you speak and then it is much easier.

It is more than just a play, it is something taken seriously. Theatre work is part of the holistic approach of Martina's pedagogy, it is responsive to the complex forms of expression of children. During the intensive process from the first rehearsal to the performance, everybody learns a lot: the theatre expands the physical, linguistic and mimic forms of expressions; children enhance their personal development with and through acting. It develops the 'creativity of the individual child and the creativity of the group' (Lenzen 1990). Apart from the work on the forms of expression (production), theatre offers possibilities to observe. Children learn pantomime and shadow play; they play with masks and learn at the same time to perceive movements and processes, to speak about them, to rearrange them. In one situation, pupils are actors, at another time they are sitting in the audience, when the others are acting, then they themselves act again. Theatre work is a code of practice of analysis, of respective systematic observation and of production. It is a creative opportunity for co production between pupils and teacher.

Conclusion

The changes at Bridge School during the last ten years show that an Austrian school can become an inspiring place for learners and teachers. A visionary head started the democratic developments, inspired by his many years of experiences in Freinet pedagogy. In regular meetings, the staff started to rethink teaching and learning, searched for forms of cooperation beyond their classrooms. The school opened itself to the wider community. The alliances beyond the school gate provided a strong political base (cp. Jeffrey and Woods 2003) and made changes possible on a large scale. Bridge School now provides a challenging place to learn and to teach and continues its developments, 'It's never finished', the head emphasises.

References

Beetlestone, F. (1998) *Creative children, imaginative teaching*, Buckingham: Open University Press.

Csikszentmihalyi, M. (1997) *Creativity*, 2nd ed. Stuttgart: Klett-Cotta.

Jeffrey, B. and Woods, P. (2003) *The creative school,*. London: Falmer.

Lenzen, K.D. (1990) *Theatre makes school*, Frankfurt am Main: Research Group Primary School.

Schratz, M., Steiner-Löffler, U. (1999) *The learning School*, 2nd ed. Weinheim und Basel: Beltz.

Woods, P. (1999) Reconstructing Progressivism. Paper read at the International Study Association for Teachers and Teaching Conference, 27-31 July, at Dublin.

Vygotsky, L. S. (1978) *Mind in Society*, Cambridge Mass. Harvard University Press.

Creative learning and possibility thinking

Bob Jeffrey and Anna Craft
The Open University, England

Research into creative learning derives from research into creative teaching. We now wish to look at creativity in learning from the learner's perspective. It involves observing how learners' develop creative opportunities and how they manipulate and reconstruct situations to engage their own creativity. The research also focuses on how learners make their creative experiences meaningful.

Research, carried out by Woods and Jeffrey (1996; Woods, et al. 1999; Woods, 1995, 1993, 1990; Jeffrey, 2001, 2003; Jeffrey and Woods, 1997, 2003) so far suggests that creative learning involves

- *relevance*. Teaching that contains this is operating within a broad range of accepted social values while being attuned to pupils' identities and cultures.
- *control of learning processes*. The pupil is self-motivated, not governed by extrinsic factors, or purely task-oriented exercises.
- *ownership of knowledge*. The pupil learns for herself—not the teacher's, examiner or society's knowledge. Creative learning is internalised, and makes a difference to the pupil's self.
- *innovation*. Something new is created. A major change has taken place—a new skill mastered, new insight gained, new understanding realised, new, meaningful knowledge acquired. A radical shift is indicated, as opposed to more gradual, cumulative learning, with which it is complementary.

Considering the relationship among these criteria, we conclude that the higher the *relevance* of teaching to children's lives, worlds, cultures and interests, the more likelihood there is that pupils will have control of their own learning processes. Relevance aids identification, motivation, excitement and enthusiasm. Control, in turn, leads to *ownership* of the knowledge that results. If relevance, control and ownership apply, the greater the chance of creative learning resulting—something new is created; there is significant change or 'transformation' in the pupil—i. e. *innovation* (Woods, 1999).

Woods and Jeffrey (1996) described teachers' strategies for achieving relevance by sharing and creating knowledge with their pupils, stimulating 'possibility knowledge' through imagination, utilising children's prior knowledge, and developing 'common knowledge' (Edwards, and Mercer, 1987). In Jeffrey and Woods (1997) student perspectives on creative teaching were discussed, showing relevance achieved by: 1. responding to pupils' emotions; 2. engaging interest by having 'fun', giving pupils ideas, stimulating imaginations; 3. maintaining pupils' individuality; 4. encouraging pupils' critical faculties.

Recent research in this area by us (Jeffrey, 2001) has found students acting creatively to enhance their learning experiences by

+ using their own experiences to enhance learning contexts;
+ using imaginative links to aid conceptualisations; creating social learning interactions with peers;
+ adding their perspectives to teacher-led lessons and
+ by offering evaluations of learning practices to improve the quality of teaching and learning.

Jeffrey and Craft (2004) identified a teaching strategy—learner inclusivity—that assists creative learning. It is an approach that includes learners in decisions about what knowledge is to be investigated, about how to investigate it and how to evaluate the learning processes (op. cit.). Teachers using this approach

+ value learners' experiences, contributions, evaluations and perspectives (Jeffrey, 2001),
+ engage in co-participative ventures with learners, (Craft, 2002; Jeffrey, 2003) and
+ develop possibility thinking (Craft, 2000, 2002)

We focus on the last of these teaching strategies. 'Possibility thinking' is part of the 'cognitive explorations' focus in the CLASP research.

Possibility thinking encompasses an attitude which refuses to be stumped by circumstances, but uses imagination, with intention, to find a way around a problem. It involves the posing of questions, whether or not these are actually conscious, formulated or voiced. The posing of questions may range from wondering about the world which surrounds us, which may lead to both finding and solving problems; and from formulated questions at one end of the spectrum, through to nagging puzzles, to a general sensitivity at the other. Possibility thinking, also involves problem finding. The ability to identify a question, a topic for investigation, a puzzle to explore or a possible new option, all involve 'finding' or 'identifying' a problem (using the word problem in a loose way, to mean 'other possibilities' (Craft, 2002).

It is a questioning way of thinking, and puzzling, asking 'what if'. It is being open to possibilities and having an exploratory attitude. It thus involves imagination and speculation (op. cit.). 'All creativity is creative thinking' (Elliot in Craft, 2002).

The research, on which this paper is based, shows how using a conception of possibility thinking gives us some insight into the nature of creative learning. The data comes from a primary school with seven classes during a special Maths week where the whole school focused on pattern and shape. Two classes visited Watford football club, specialist PE teachers gave lessons on shape, two classes visited the local secondary school to use some of their maths apparatus, all the children took part in a sponsored 'mathelon' to raise money for the Great Ormond Street Children's hospital in London and they had a maths trail one afternoon where the classes circulated round to every teacher carrying out a different maths activity in each. The week finished with a report to a special assembly of parents. The teachers provided special maths sessions and topics for the week and they found the whole exercise a welcome opportunity to be creative themselves. The opportunity to teach is a major factor in the development of teaching creatively (Woods, 1990) and the opportunity to learn is also crucial for the development of creative learning.

Creative learning and possibility thinking

Creative learning is where learning is relevant to the learner, where they have a considerable amount of ownership and control over the materials, techniques and processes of an engagement with some knowledge or skills activity and where the opportunity to be innovative exists. Creativity can't be taught, only the conditions created to encourage it (Smith, 1975). Creative learning involves the experience of dynamic atmospheres (Jeffrey, and Woods, 2003) climates of anticipation and expectation (Jeffrey, 1996), the generation of emotional expression (Woods, 1993) and development of understandings, skills, processes, appreciation and thinking.

Creative thinking is just one of the set of thinking skills identified by the National Curriculum, the others being: information processing, reasoning, enquiry and evaluation (Wegerif, 2002) although they are also involved in creative thinking. The latter has been characterised as tearing up and building (Beetlestone, 1998), as imagining, investigating, anticipating, organising, and control of ideas and judgements (Halliwell, 1993), collaborations (Cocklin, et al. 1996), physical and mental togetherness, making predictions, co-operations, creating one's own assumptions, associative collaboration with peers (Dowrick, 1993), playing with ideas, possibilities and evaluations, (N.A.C.C.C., 1999), the freedom to investigate, make mistakes and to choose (Reggio Emilia, 1996).

Possibility thinking is a particular part of the process of creative thinking. The instigators of the Reggio Emilia educational programme for young children maintain that children are born with all the languages of life. These languages are interactive by nature and are equipped with the exploratory and perceptive tools for seeking out exchange and reciprocity. 'They embody the incipient art of the semiologist and the detective, the ability to use investigative methods, to hypothesise 'missing' explanations and reconstruct facts ... the more languages we recognise in children, the more we can help them act and identify the methodological models they need for confronting events and experience so as to absorb Olsen's anomalies, Bateson's differences, or Piaget's schemas in as constructive process that is applicable to all learning. And this gives strength to the children's own projects and desires.' (op. cit.)

Possibility thinking is a situation where the learner either takes control of an exploration, investigation or problem or collaborates with others in the same processes. Possibility thinking is creative where it involves an exploration of resources, ideas, mediums and patterns, for example, weaving possibilities, collage activities and tessellations. These explorations are open adventures.

Possibility thinking is creative when learners investigate the possible techniques for identifying the properties of materials or the processes to arrive at a numerical pattern such as triangular numbers. It is not the outcome of these investigations that is creative but the innovative ways in which learners process the investigation, creativity is a process not the event (N.A.C.C.C.E., 1999). Year 5 had to create an Aztec container by constructing a 3D net. There were many different solutions but the process was framed by the instruction to create a geometric net. These investigations are open tasks.

Problem solving engages possibility thinking in seeking solutions with an outcome focused approach. Ideas and strategies are posed, discussed, experimented with and evaluated. The drawing of a house with a computer programme without lifting the pen from the screen is an example, as is, how to count a large number of dots on a piece of paper. The creative processes involve 'what if' questions and the innovative strategies used to solve the problem. Problem solving is, in this case, solution seeking.

Possibility thinking in the process of creative learning occurs in open adventures, (explorations), open tasks (investigations) and solution seeking (problem solving). Possibility thinking is the action of bringing a new idea or process to the situation.

Central to the opportunity for possibility thinking is the kind of context created by teachers. Teaching creatively leads to teaching for creativity (N.A.C.C.C. 1999) just as providing the appropriate resources aids possibility thinking for learners as in this example where *manipulation,* one of the features of possibility thinking, was significant.

The Year 4 learners were given white boards and felt tip pens to design cover slides for their topic books. In the Victorian age children used slates and chalk and we have leapfrogged the less efficient period when we used pencils and rubbers to white boards for this creative use of resources.

They then all went into the computer suite and had about twenty minutes to prepare a presentation of a couple of slides. The computer suite was impressive. It consisted of three hexagonal workstations over a metre high with the children sitting on high chairs sharing a computer between two of them. It was in a light airy room with lots of computer designs and relevant vocabulary spread around the walls. The hexagonal workstations were similar to the central control panel in the Doctor Who's Tardis and the head teacher told me it had specifically been designed to be attractive to young learners. The design encouraged the children to consult and collaborate with each other easily. Learners pressed their fingers to their lips as they gazed at the screens exhibiting puzzled brows balancing on the edges of their stools as they slowly revolved them backwards and forwards. One hand covered the mouse with a constantly twitching forefinger stabbing at its shoulder and the other hand occasionally dabbed at the screen or searched for an appropriate button. They debated and evaluated choices, quality and techniques.

As the teacher demonstrated some of the dynamic actions of this programme, such as how to get words and phrases spiralling on to the screen, I could see how these movements were similar to cartoons. The learners seemed to like the dynamism of a virtual environment where clicks opened menus which were scrolled and trawled and thrown into the ether with another click.   (Field Note, 19 March 2003)

During the maths week, on which this research draws its data, the resources used were extensive providing a context suitable for open adventures, open tasks and solution seeking.

Open adventures

Learners have personal connections or individual ideas that give relevance to their learning experiences (Jeffrey, B. and Woods, P. 1997). James (Year 6) was asked why he was trying out different pictures with his tangram pieces before deciding which one to select and he narrated the reasons for his approach:

> Because I like being creative. I like making different pictures and drawings, and sketches because I have got a good imagination. When I draw I come out with queer ideas like space ships and when writing a story I think about the future and then I have a story. My mum has told me that I'm imaginative. I'll make anything that nobody else has made. I go a bit crazy drawing a scientist holding a test tube and getting his face blown up.

Learners bring their experiences, observations and imagination to the classroom to make learning relevant and they also make contributions to the teaching and learning process. One way of doing this using possibility thinking is to make comparisons. While listening to details of how to construct a mosaic in Year 3 one boy suggested that 'it's like doing a tangram—following a trail and taking time.'

Control is a major feature of all creative teaching and learning and learners exercise this control as often as they can in learning activities. This control, which is either wrested from young people or negotiated away by them for other benefits such as love, status, self-esteem and more material offerings, is a major element of the creative enterprise (Jeffrey, B. and Craft, A. 2004). Constructing pictures from a tangram means *experimenting*, a form of possibility thinking,

> Jake makes a duck, then an Elvis picture, then a duck's head and a funnel followed by a chimney. 'I'm seeing what I can make. I don't decide beforehand. "I've decided on the dinosaur. It's interesting and it's the best of all I have done. It's the most creative.'   (Field Note, 19 May 2003)

However, different approaches show how possibilities can be located in open imagination as in the example above or by pre-selecting a frame:

> Cloe tries to make a 'spooky' picture because the background picture is black. 'Does it look like a ghost? It's floating. It has a tail like some ghosts and these are the arms like wings helping them to fly. I'm going to do

a spider. It's hanging from there. I decided to make it because you find them in spooky places.   (Field Note, 19 May 2003)

These examples show the different methods used to decide what picture to do. Jake goes for the 'make a lot and then decide approach' and Cloe decides on a framework and a more instantaneous approach is taken by James. He constructed a design and then used his imagination to determine its constituency.

I have made a sign that goes on a 'baby changing door'. It struck me straight away. It's my first choice and it looked real. It looks like a baby holder, like a clip.

These three examples show experimentation, framework development and instantaneous ideas to be features of possibility thinking in an exploratory context.

Risk taking is also part of the exploratory adventure. Young people experiment from an early age and young learners often want to continue to push boundaries at the same time as they become more aware of the consequences of taking risks. They might affect status, confidence, self-esteem, peer and teacher relations but, for some, it is still worth doing if the process leads to innovative opportunities. The Year 4 children had taken pictures of themselves on a digital camera in their computer club and put it onto a *Dazzle* file. They then worked on reconstructing their friend's picture.

Hannah: I made her weird and made her crazy and put weird clothes on her. I put a beard on her and big cracked yellow ears and purple hair with blue spots and I put a crown on her big hair do. She thinks it's disgusting. She'll say "Tara, you're going crazy" as I put on a funny blue nose and weird black eyes.
Hannah: Tara made it crazy. It's funny. If I did look like that I would freak out.
Tara: I like being horrible. It's really fun making people weird. It's funny when you print it out. You would say 'What have I done to Hannah. Look at her. She's weird'.
Tara: Hannah, I think you have made me absolutely disgusting. I hate it.

Hannah: I made it disgusting. I made the scriggly bogies go on her silky dress. The eyes are in different places. That's why there are three. It is turning into a monster and her hands are creaky and freaking,
(Field Note, 20 May 2003).

Taking risks with their friendships is adventurous and dangerous but it would appear that their creative juices have taken control. It may be that it is because they are re-presenting their friends that they feel secure to do something so outrageous. Either way they enjoyed the activity immensely at the same time as experimenting with the technology and a wide range of possibility designs.

Possibility thinking can also be co-participative. The Year 3 children are planning a mosaic with some clay tiles. The teacher drew a four by four square on a white board and talked about making a design with two to three colours.

> The children used felt tips and halved or even quartered the squares and coloured them differently to make a shape or pattern. One boy asked if the class are going to make one large one. Sonia said 'It's a good idea and they may do it later in the week'. Another asked if they could 'cover them in PVA glue to make them shiny'. 'Yes, if you think that they are not shiny enough' replied the teacher.   (Field Note, 20 May 2003)

The children come out to the white board one by one and begin to fill up the example, one square at a time, following other patterns and introducing new elements, e. g. dots, circles, spirals, wavy lines, stripes/colours. Sonia asks for other ideas after a little while of experimenting. Ashben (a profoundly deaf child) says 'I would do a row of red and then a row of blue keeping it simple. Another suggests interlocked triangles. They are all given a piece of squared paper and they draw a 4 x 4 square on it.

> One learner produces a very symmetrical with four shapes and 4 colours. Another tries to do a dinosaur. Another includes all the shapes arbitrarily. Another divides all the squares in two diagonally then puts in different designs in each. Another does a mixture of objects. Another colours them in green and blue. Another does a face.

One boy says 'I was doing a stream of blue and then it looked like the sea so I added the seaside with some yellow and the sun'.

When the class are together again the teachers offers them an opportunity to show the class and explain their creations. Where she is unsure as to whether a design will work she says 'let's wait and see'.

(Field Note, 20 March 2003)

The exploration began with a collection of possibilities and discussion of them. Some of the learners drew on ideas developed in the joint session, others on the framework provided and others on instantaneous ideas.

Open tasking

Investigations are more specific tasks which employ possibility thinking, although it may be spontaneous possibility thinking that begins the open tasking.

One of the Foundation teachers reminded a learner not to 'wear your jumper round your stomach. It looks untidy'. Amy said 'And it might squeeze your blood and bones. It might make your blood go up and up and up to your ear and explode like it did to my sister. It came out of her ears but it might also come out of a scratch'. The class then explored the nature of blood flow, and described explosions by drawing some on the whiteboard. The learners drew arms being thrown into the air.

(Field Note, 22 May 2003)

Frameworks are often built into open tasking by the teacher rather than chosen by the learner as in the open adventures. Creative choice tempered by patterning limits and technical possibilities still left control in the learners' hands as evidenced by a weaving activity in Year 3. Emily 'chose to weave red and white because it makes a pattern and matches, the colours go together and the patterns have to repeat'. Creative learning arises from the interaction of classroom pedagogy and the culture. Open tasking usually results in different outcomes or no outcomes at all.

One of the challenges during the Maths trail around different classes was to see how far the learners could get doubling numbers, without calculators. Daniel (Year 5) starts at 110 'because I like a challenge. It doesn't matter if I don't finish'. In this case the finished product is not a requirement nor a focus, the process itself is seen as enough of challenge to engage learners and Daniel used his control over the process to take ownership of the task by starting where he wanted to and to determine its success criteria.   (Field Note, 21 June 2003)

Learners are keen to develop complexity as well as challenges. Year 5 learners were given the task of developing star shapes by drawing lines between six equidistance points on a circle during the Maths Trail,

> 'Its fun seeing how far you can get, putting in more lines and making it more complex'; 'The colouring is less important than making a complex pattern'.   (Year 5) (Field Note, 23 June 2003)

Constructing the contexts for possibility thinking or possibility thinking itself encourages the construction of creative habits such as developing complexity and simplicity as Jamie observed after completing his collaged faceplate:

> The plate pattern I have done is too complicated. I wanted to see how many shapes I could make. I've made new shapes. I have to name them. This one is an oval and this is a triangle. This one starts like an oval but it loops round. There are loads of triangles. If I do it again I think I'll do it differently, simpler, it's too complicated. There are bits coming out of it everywhere. It's been quite hard but enjoyable. I would still enjoy a simpler one. I wouldn't have to attach the bits with *sellotape* to keep them on. It would still be satisfying, simpler but not so many bits.

Possibility thinking is to be found in the process of open tasking, even in more instrumental tasks.

> The Year 6 teacher spent twenty minutes going through their homework, which was to find as many words that began with aqua-, octo-, tri-, trans-, anni-, and sent-. One child managed to find over 600 and it must have taken her a lot of hours. However, in the process of class discussion it became clear that she had used a variety of sources including the internet.   (Field Note, 17 March 2003)

There followed a co-participative investigation of the nature of 'pop art'.

> She accepted all contributions offered and recorded them on her white
> board. Her pedagogic style was not 'elicitation'—displaying what one
> wished to be recorded by choosing the appropriate comments from the
> children. She accepted all the contributions but she emphasised the
> one she thought was correct and relevant. Some of the children have
> developed a style of asking if a possibility might be correct—possibility
> thinking and possibility knowledge. She then showed them some pictures
> from a book of Pop Art and established some general conception of it
> through discussion. (op. cit.)

Possibility thinking had become part of the general culture of this classroom
and in doing so each contribution and idea held its value until it fell out of use
or it was superseded by others. Possibility thinking as a form of investigation
itself had been employed. The investigation above turned into a solution seeking
activity when the learners then went to the IT suite to construct a drawing of
a seaside picture using a pop art.

Solution seeking

The possibilities employed in the process of solution seeking are only bounded
by the parameters of the problem to be solved but the final outcome is predetermined, although different forms might be produced. Foundation learners
used possibility thinking to produce a firework on the *Dazzle* software in the
ICT suite.

> *Neve*: We don't want some white.
> *Melissa*: We can go over it.
> *Azone*: With red.
> *Melissa*: I'll throw it away and now I'll put it back. It won't go.
> *Neve*: I'll do another. Your turn Azone.
> *Azone*: Your turn Melissa.
> *Never*: I'll put it back for you: there.
> *Azone*: You're making the whole page go pink.
> *Melissa*: I'll get it back.
> *Azone*: Let's have some blue on it.
> *Teacher*: Try to use the same colour with different shades.

Azone: We could do another.

Neve: With different colours or shall we dump it and start again. I'll put it into the bin. I'll kiss it goodbye.

The learners experimented with colour and form and with 'repeat starts', *a recursive aspect* of possibility thinking.

The learners in Year 4 were working on Pascal's triangle in which the sum of the numbers at the end of each line of the developing triangle adds up to, what are known as the triangular numbers, e. g.: $1+2=3$; $1+2+3=6$; $1+2+3+4=10$; etc. There is a pattern to the differences between the triangular numbers, i. e.: add 2 then 3 then 4 to the last total; the next triangular number after 10 is $10+5$, then $15+6$. Seb commented 'its fun adding up and finding patterns between numbers. It's good finding a pattern in the position of the numbers. It's a finished piece, a masterpiece'.

There is an element of discovery in seeking solutions which feed feelings of excitement and pleasure and also of ownership and control but if it does not involve innovation the process is less creative. Where the process encourages innovation, such as the construction of patterns for design or as part of the process of problem solving, then the activity can be seen as creative.

> Others took the problem of making as many sums by only using digits 1, 2, 3. One girl observed that 'You make them up as you go along but you have to think. I learnt to use patterns e. g.: $23+1$; $23+2$; $23+3$; $23+3+1$; $23+3+2$; $23+3+3$; $23+3+3+1$; $23+3+3+2$; $23+3+3+3$.
>
> (Field Note, 21 May 2003)

Patterning is either an outcome of possibility thinking employed across the first three characteristics of learning or is used as a strategy for problem solving.

Problem solving, like excitement and pleasure can only be considered a major element of creative learning if there is an element of innovativeness in the process. Year 5 were asked to estimate how many grains of sand on a picture and to provide details of the methods used to solve the problem: 'I counted the grains of sand in a small area and then multiplied the number of small areas'; 'I did columns and rows'; 'I put a line across and down and multiplied'; 'I circled and counted the number in each circle'; and 'I think I had about a 100 cubes of sand'.

Across open adventures, open tasking and solution seeking these learners have employed a range of possibility thinking features—manipulation, comparison, experimentation, framework development, instantaneous ideas, risk taking, co-participation, complexity development, simplicity extraction, recursiveness and patterning. Where these involved innovation creative learning was experienced and enacted.

Creative learning: the learner's perspective.

Encouraging possibility thinking as part of a 'learner inclusive' approach during this maths week at the case study school, generated learners' knowledge about learning itself and highlighted the nature of learning processes. Year 5s evaluation of the competencies gained from constructing their Aztec box included: 'It is how to design something and not mess it up, to reduce the failure rate and to make a box with tabs'; 'We learnt scoring and cutting skills, how to draw accurately, improve computation skills, folding skills, manipulating scissors and practising measuring'. They were also knowledgeable about the nature of learning.

> We discussed the difference between 'natural'/unintentional learning—how to be untidy and school/intentional learning: 'You just do it'; 'Learning at school is learning how'; 'Natural learning is easy, this learning is also easy'; 'It includes failure and practise and thinking'; 'It includes strategies, different skills and different ways of doing things'; 'We need to think about what we are trying to do'; 'We are conscious of something in our minds'; 'Learning is a step towards something. I am learning that you make mistakes and then practice'; Learning involves planning like experimenting and being briefed first'   (Field Note, 20 May 2003).

Learners also understand the relationship between learning and achievement. When asked if there are subjects that they like but in which they are not so competent Sophie (Year 3) said, 'I like Literacy because of the writing. I'm not good at science but I like the experiments, however I struggle to understand it sometimes'. David (Year 3) said, 'I don't like writing stories. I like bike riding and football but I am not good at them'.

A sample of the Year 6 learners had evaluated national assessment procedures and concluded that, in general, they were mostly unruffled by national tests (future paper) but they recommended other forms of assessments that could be used—communicative competencies, collaborative qualities and management of knowledge, e. g. individual project folders. Learners 'speak the discourse' (Ball, 1994) and to that extent, like any adult, they are able to engage in discussion and analysis of learning and assessment (Jeffrey, 2001, 2003).

Further, the inclusion of possibility thinking in classroom activities has a direct effect on learners' appreciation of creative learning. The Year 5 learners valued the open task of constructing the Aztec nets because it provided opportunities for individual ownership, control and innovation possibilities. Their evaluations included:

> 'Becoming your own teacher, teaching yourself'; 'Choosing the way you want to do it'; 'Choosing is important because you choose the best way of doing it. You know yourself better than others'. You can choose your own level, less challenging and more challenging. Some of us want harder things. I am proud of not being like everyone else. It belongs to you. You own it'; 'You can do what you want to do. You achieve something that was good'.   (Field Note, 20 May 2004)

Making the activities relevant to them stimulated their creativity and celebrating their reasons for making decisions and the diversity of their individual strategies is an important teaching strategy for developing and maintaining creative learning. Being encouraged to pose questions, identify problems and issues together with the opportunity to debate and discuss their 'thinking' brings the learner into the process of possibility thinking as a co-participant (Reggio Emilia, 1996).

Conclusion

Possibility thinking can become a *creative habit* as was exemplified in Year 6 where learners often posed possibilities whole in class activities and in examples of learner explorations, investigations and the processes of seeking solutions. It is one of the one hundred languages of children developed at an early age, which they renew in a recursive way (Jeffrey, and Craft, 2003) when learning contexts are conducive. Its grammar is the features outlined above and its syntax is seen in the discussions between learners and teachers and learners as well as the organising processes that make up the explorations, investigations and problem solving.

It is a language that may be invoked by teacher or learner at any time or one that is highlighted as a major strategy. It is a language that stimulates creativity and is used to translate learning experiences into creative learning. Moreover it is an inclusive language that brings learners together either in a specific task or as a community of practice (Lave, and Wenger, 1991).

References

Ball, S. J. (1994) *Education reform: A critical and post-structural approach.* Buckingham: Open University Press.

Beetlestone, F. (1998) *Creative children, imaginative teaching.* Buckingham: Open University Press.

Cocklin, B. Coombe, K. and Retallick, J. (1996) Learning communities in education: Directions for professional development. Paper read at *British Educational Research Association Conference*, 12-15 September, at Lancaster.

Craft, A. (2000) *Creativity across the primary curriculum: Framing and developing practice*: London: Routledge.

Craft, A. (2002) *Creativity and early years education.* London: Continuum.

Craft, A. and Jeffrey, B. (2004) Creative practice and practice which fosters creativity in Miller, L. and Devereux, J., *Supporting Children's Learning in the Early Years*, London; David Fulton Publishers

Dowrick, N. (1993) Side by side: A more appropriate form of peer interaction for infant pupils, *British Educational Research Journal* 19 (5):499-515.

N.A.C.C.C.E. (1999) *All our futures: Creativity, culture and education.* London: Department for Employment and Education.

Edwards, D. and Mercer, N. (1987) *Common knowledge: The development of understanding in classrooms,* London: Methuen.

Reggio Emilia (1996) *The hundred languages of children,* Reggio Emilia: Reggio Children.

Halliwell, S. (1993) Teacher creativity and teacher education, in Bridges, D. and Kerry, T. (eds) *Developing teachers professionally,* London: Routledge.

Jeffrey, B. (1996) Creating tone and atmosphere in primary classrooms, in Chawla-Duggan, R. and Pole, C. J. (eds) *Reshaping education in the 1990s: Perspectives on primary schooling,* London: Falmer Press.

Jeffrey, B. (2001). Primary pupil's perspectives and creative learning. *Encyclopaideia* (Italian Journal) 9 (Spring):133-152.

Jeffrey, B. (2003) Countering student instrumentalism: A creative response. *British Educational Research Journal* 29 (4): 489-504.

Jeffrey, B. and Craft, A. (2004) Creative teaching and teaching for creativity: Distinctions and relationships. *Educational Studies,* 30(1): 77-87

Jeffrey, B., and Woods, P. (1997) The relevance of creative teaching: Pupils' views, in Pollard, A. Thiessen, D. and Filer, A. (eds) *Children and their curriculum: The perspectives of primary and elementary children,* London: Falmer.

Jeffrey, B. and Woods, P. (2003) *The creative school: A framework for success, quality and effectiveness,* London: Routledge/Falmer.

Lave, J. and Wenger, E. (1991) *Situated learning: Legitimate peripheral participation,* New York: Cambridge University Press.

Smith, J. A. (1975) *Creative teaching of reading in the elementary school,* Boston: Allyn and Bacon

Wegerif, R. (2003) Literature Review in Thinking Skills, Technology and Learning, Nesta Futurelab, www.nestafuturelab.org

Woods, P. (1990) *Teacher skills and strategies*, London, Falmer.

Woods, P. (1993) *Critical events in teaching and learning*, London: Falmer Press.

Woods, P. (1995) *Creative teachers in primary schools*, Buckingham: Open University Press.

Woods, P. (1999) Reconstructing progressivism, Paper read at *ISATT Conference,* at Dublin, July.

Woods, P. Boyle, M., and Hubbard, N. (1999) *Multicultural children in the early years.* Clevedon: Multilingual Matters

Woods, P. and Jeffrey, B. (1996) *Teachable moments: The art of creative teaching in primary schools,* Buckingham: Open University Press.

Bilingual learners' perspectives on school and society in Scotland

Geri Smyth
University of Strathclyde

Introduction

The dispersal of around 1,200 children from asylum seeking families to Glasgow's schools resulted in the setting up of the Glasgow Asylum Seekers Support Project (GASSP) funded by National Asylum Seekers' Support (NASS). The educational wing of this project established bilingual units in schools across Glasgow, in which specialist teachers would support the English language development of the newly arrived pupils while enabling their integration into the mainstream classes by team teaching.

The project provides clear support guidelines for teachers in the bilingual bases, which prioritise responsive teaching and learning strategies over curriculum. Thus the rationale for educational provision for children from asylum seeking families (GASSP 2001) urges schools and teachers to take into account breaks in education (experienced by the children) and English as an Additional Language (EAL) needs, based on existing best practice. The GASSP rationale for the curriculum states it must be guided by principles of good practice in bilingual education and cites references to the research that identifies good practice. Children and teachers are at the heart of this rationale rather than a curriculum, societal needs or performativity policies. The aim of the support provided by the teachers in the bilingual bases is to integrate pupils into mainstream classes and so the teachers work with existing schemes of work. However, where aspects of existing curriculum materials are inappropriate, the teachers find innovative ways of achieving the same outcomes. Such an approach may help to liberate teachers, and thus children, from the constraints of a curriculum driven approach to education and may enable researchers to identify ways in which teachers help to make learning relevant for children, a key feature identified by Woods (1990) in providing creative teaching.

Context

Sample

The Glasgow CLASP research was conducted in one primary school, Lady Jane Grey. Lady Jane Grey primary school is a three-storey red sandstone Victorian school building in the centre of a housing scheme in the city of Glasgow. The school is surrounded by high-rise flats built in the late 1960s and now due for demolition. There is large-scale deprivation in the area marked by high rates of crime, illegal drug use and suicide. This housing scheme is now one in which Glasgow City Council have chosen to house dispersed asylum seeker families as they await the Home Office decision as to their status. Consequently, the school, which until recently had very few non-white, non-monolingual English speaking pupils, now has almost a hundred pupils from Somalia, the Congo, Sri Lanka, Turkey, Afghanistan, Iran, Iraq, Pakistan, the Lebanon, Zimbabwe, Russia and Lithuania. These children, by dint of having to use English for the purposes of education in the classroom and using at least one other language at home to communicate with their families, can be deemed bilingual (Wiles, 1985). There are a total of 200 pupils in the school, aged five to twelve-years-old.

The school has a bilingual base which employs four teachers in addition to the seven mainstream classes. All newly arrived children from asylum seeking families (and other bilingual children) are registered with an age appropriate mainstream class. They all go to their register class at the start of the day and attend this class for art, drama, music, physical education, religious education, science, technology, health education and social subjects. They are taught in the bilingual base for maths and language until the base teachers and mainstream teachers together assess that they have enough English to be able to work within the mainstream classroom. The children with very little English also have an hour a day in the base for 'reception time' to improve their English. The teachers from the base team teach in the mainstream classrooms for part of the time. All teachers in the school participate in running after school clubs for the children, e. g. computer, art, netball, football etc. In these ways, the teachers from the bilingual base are not viewed by the pupils as only being there to support the bilingual pupils.

Creative Learning and Bilingual Pupils

As earlier stated, the children in the Glasgow CLASP study were all bilingual and I wished to investigate the ways in which they dealt with an unfamiliar curriculum delivered in an unfamiliar language. I found that the methodology employed by the GASSP teachers and supported by the mainstream staff and school management team, led, in this school to the existence of a daily multilingual conference, with the bilingual children as active participants in this conference, resulting in their taking ownership of the new curriculum and language.

The underlying hypothesis concerning creative thinking and bilingualism is that the ownership of two or more languages may increase fluency, flexibility, originality and elaboration in thinking. This is derived from an understanding that bilinguals will have two or more words for a single object or idea and this will allow a person more freedom and richness of thought. International and cross cultural research has compared bilinguals and monolinguals on a variety of measures of divergent thinking (Ricciardelli, 1992) and found bilinguals to be largely superior to monolinguals, although this has been mostly in additive bilingual contexts (Lauren, 1991). Cummins, (1977) proposed that

> There may be a threshold level of linguistic competence which a bilingual child must attain both in order to avoid cognitive deficits and allow the potentially beneficial aspects of becoming bilingual to influence his cognitive growth.

Studies reported by Ricciardelli (1992) that did not support bilingual superiority in divergent thinking sampled less proficient bilinguals, a result consistent with Cummins' Threshold Theory.

The bilingual pupils in my study were not balanced bilinguals, as they were not equally fluent in both their languages across contexts. Nor were they in an additive bilingual situation (Lambert, 1980) as they were acquiring an additional language in a situation where their first language was expected to be replaced. Did this mean then that their bilingualism would not enhance their creativity? Woods et al. (1999) had considered the creativity of young bilingual children although their pupils had been four to five years-old and born in the United Kingdom. Would the six to twelve-year-old children from asylum seeking families recently arrived in Scotland and with very little English demonstrate any of the features of creative learning as identified by Woods (1990) i.e. innovation, ownership of knowledge, control of the learning processes and relevance of the curriculum? If so, what features of the teaching in the school would enable this creative learning to take place?

The Education of Bilingual Pupils in Scotland

There is currently no national policy for the education of bilingual pupils and this can lead to confusion amongst teachers as to what is the best practice to adopt. The development of a policy through the GASSP project has enabled mainstream teachers to see good practice in action and has had an impact on their understandings and practices as will be highlighted in this paper.

English for Immigrants (DES, 1963) was the first major government intervention into the teaching of children whose first language was not English. The language needs of the newly arrived immigrant population of schools were addressed only in relation to the perceived need for education for the white monolingual majority pupils not to be disrupted by their presence. The cultural needs of the immigrant population were not addressed in official policy and this legacy remains today.

Educational responses to the existence of children whose first language was not English have varied (Mills and Mills, 1993) with initial responses to the education of bilingual children in Britain being focused on assimilation as quickly as possible into the so-called 'host community', ignoring children's specific language needs. As concern grew about the under-achievement of ethnic minority pupils in British schools (DES, 1985) responses developed into practices ranging from teaching bilingual pupils in separate language centres to withdrawing such children from their mainstream classes for the purposes of specialist English language tuition (Bourne, 1990; Herriman and Burnaby, 1996). This tuition often bore little or no relation to the child's curriculum in class. All these educational responses ignored the existence of the children's first language. (Mills and Mills 1993)

Since the 1980s the preferred approach has been to teach English language to children for whom it is an additional language in the context of other learning within the mainstream classroom (Wiles, 1985; SCCC 1994). This puts demands on the classroom teacher to carefully consider the language needs of the bilingual child in relation to the content of classroom teaching.

Stubbs (1994) argues that 'schools have always been the most powerful mechanism in assimilating minority children into mainstream cultures'. His analysis of the work of the committees which have produced statements on language in the education system for England and Wales concludes that this burgeoning of ad-hoc language planning has created a 'sophisticated control which recognises ethnic diversity but confines it to the home, which pays lip-service to multilingualism but is empty liberal rhetoric.'

Thompson, Fleming and Byram (1996) similarly suggest that UK government language policy may be discerned and analysed by considering the recommendations of official committees of enquiry into the education of speakers of languages other than English, or into the teaching of English in schools. Bourne (1990) provides a detailed historical overview of the changes in language policy as expressed in *The Bullock Report* (DES, 1975), *The Swann Report* (DES, 1985), *The Harris Report* (DES, 1990) and *The Cox Report* (DES, 1989) the latter resulting in the National Curriculum for English. These responses are particular to England and Wales, although all the named reports have had an influence on the situation in Scotland.

Bourne (1997) stresses that in the changing context of British education the support of bilingual children in the mainstream requires a radical rethinking of policy. She is referring specifically to the effects in England and Wales of the 1988 Education Act, the National Curriculum and league tables but her arguments apply equally to the evolution in Scotland of the 5-14 Curriculum Guidelines, National Testing, Best Value assessment and Target Setting.

There is no language policy in the United Kingdom which explicitly states that home languages other than English should be eradicated but nor is there an official policy document relating to the promotion of home languages.

Stubbs (1994) argues that language planning in Britain has been conducted by separate isolated committees with split consultation procedures and with different working groups having been responsible for developing guidelines for different areas of the curriculum.

In this complex situation of limited national policy and conflicting government reports, teachers have to resort to their common sense beliefs, or folk theories about how best to teach bilingual pupils. In Smyth's (2001) research, mainstream teachers' folk theories about the place of bilingualism in education were found to be similar across the sample. However, practices in that study Smyth (2001) were found to relate not only to the teachers' beliefs but also to what support systems for bilingual pupils were available in the different authorities. The absence of policy and the differentiated provision in the authorities was found to be a major factor in the adoption of disparate opinions and practices and, in some cases, lowered expectations of the bilingual pupils.

Creative Teaching and Bilingual pupils

How then can teachers adopt creative teaching practices with pupils whom they are unsure how to teach? Woods (1990) suggests that one of the empirical features of creative teaching is the relevance of the curriculum and teaching practices that operate within a broad range of accepted social values while being attuned to students' identities and cultures. Woods et al. (1999) propose that the relevance of values and context is especially significant in the teaching of bilingual children as a critical factor in creative teaching. They suggest that this relevance is manifested particularly in the encouragement of children's free play, in activities that start from the child; in the development of home-school links; and in the teaching that occurs 'in the margins' of programmed activity and through spontaneous reaction to children's interests.

Cummins (1996) writes that, 'human relationships are central to effective instruction—particularly in the case of second language learners who may be trying to find their way in the borderlands between cultures'. While not explicitly mentioning relevance here, Cummins goes on to write that, 'for students to invest their sense of self, their identity, in acquiring their new language and participating actively in their new culture, they must experience positive and affirming interactions with members of that culture'.

Bentley, (2001) proposes a number of ways in which schools need to be restructured into learning communities and to develop abilities and forms of creativity which resonate with the twenty-first century, including 'the ability to transfer what one learns across different contexts and real world outcomes so that creativity and motivation are reinforced by the experience of making an impact and giving benefit to others'.

What makes teaching relevant?

If the knowledge conveyed to children by teachers is relevant to their concerns and reflects their societal and cultural knowledge, then it will be more easily internalised by the child and turned into personal knowledge (Woods and Jeffrey, 1996). However the societal and cultural knowledge of bilingual pupils is not prominent in the curricular guidelines for teaching in Scotland. So relevant teaching occurs where teachers strive, often against the prescribed curriculum, to construct knowledge that is meaningful within the child's frame of reference. Teachers use strategies to share and create knowledge through imagination and children's prior knowledge. Woodhead, (1995) has criticised the belief that the curriculum should be relevant to the immediate needs and interests of pupils and argues, rather, that the curriculum should provide pupils with the knowledge and skills they need to function effectively in adult working life. However, a relevance to the immediate needs and interests of pupils, especially pupil cultures, is an essential aid to achieving that effective adult state. This need for relevance was recognised by the teachers at Lady Jane Grey:

I think every single day and every single lesson I try to make it relevant for the children. I mean, I cater completely to the children's needs, which I never did as a mainstream teacher; it's a completely different style of teaching. I mean from the moment they step in the door I am thinking about how I can expand their vocabulary, how I can help them to understand just every part of school life, moving around the school, getting used to living in Scotland, you know.

(Dawn, Primary 1 Bilingual Base Teacher)

Establishing Relevance through Play:

So how did Dawn and the other teachers in Lady Jane Grey 'make it relevant for the children'? Much has been written about the benefits of play in learning to enable children to develop knowledge through practical experience. Writing about play, however, tends to focus on young children's learning strategies (e. g. Bruce, 1991; Meek, 1985; Moyles, 1989). Teachers in Lady Jane Grey, however are convinced of the need for play throughout the school, although Jane, the Bilingual Base Team Leader, recognises that play itself can sometimes constrain creativity if it is too structured:

I was going to say games were creative there but they were and they weren't. The games are probably so structured there isn't much room there for creative thought. ... that game we were playing earlier with the Six Blind Men and the Elephant was purely a reading game. I want them to be able to read the text ... So I wouldn't say there's much creative thought goes into being able to do that so it would tend to be more activities that are open. (Jane)

Jackie, the Primary 6 (ten to eleven-year-olds) class teacher, recognised the need for active involvement and acknowledged that this is what the children wanted in order to make the learning relevant to them.

It is hard to let go as an adult and turn around and say, 'Right, you're in charge, what do you want to learn, what do you want to do?' But once you find out what kids want to learn it turns out it's pretty much what you want them to learn, it's just we're going to go around it a different way, they don't want chalk and talk at the blackboard, sitting still listening to me, they want to stand up and do things.

Jane used making games as a strategy for the children to demonstrate knowledge about the local environment and discovered that the children had considerably more cultural capital than she did when it came to a knowledge of games. They wanted to go much further than she had anticipated.

> When we were making games about Palace Park and my introduction was completely basic. You know here's a wee Snakes and Ladders game and here's a Matching Pairs game. What would you come up with? And they came up with fantastic *Harry Potter* adventures and I was like, 'Oh, that's good'. They are much better creative thinkers than me 'cos I couldn't do this ... and I think a lot of the bilingual kids got involved.

For bilingual learners of all ages, play optimises use of their first language, enables them to bring their own cultural knowledge and understanding to bear and enables collaboration with others. The children in this study however were not passive recipients of instructions to play, but initiated play as a way to make sense of a new language and a new curriculum. The teachers had provided them with a stimulus that they then took control of and developed in ways in which the teachers could not have predicted.

Establishing relevance through Pupil Agency

On a visit to Palace Park with the Primary 2/3 (five to seven-year-olds) bilingual base, the children were keen to make the unfamiliar environment relevant to their existing knowledge. The purpose of the walk was a bug (insect) hunt, related to their environmental studies project on mini-beasts.

As we walked from the path beside the allotments to the park itself, a boy said, 'It's the jungle'. This resulted in many of the children making jungle noises and moving stealthily rather than walking along in pairs behind the teacher. The initial purpose of the walk seemed to have been forgotten by the children. As we emerged into the more open space of the park, the children were fascinated by the wild flowers, making buttercups shine under each other's chins and making daisy chains and comparing the lengths. When we sat down at the river one of the children picked up little stones and started playing Fives. A girl said about this game, 'I play this every day in Turkey'. The children used French, Somali and Turkish to communicate the different rules there could be for this game.

'The morning becomes less of a bug hunt and more of a day in the park: playing, exploring the environment, enjoying each others' company and the open air'.   (Lady Jane Grey Field Notes, 2 June, 2003)

Teachers may be reluctant to describe classroom activities as play, due to the over-emphasis on play as a medium for learning for younger children. Play can also be seen however as exploratory interactions between children and adults (Woods et al, 1999), perhaps fostered by the adults, but developed by the children into meaningful activity.

The school Art Club went for a series of workshops to the Lighthouse (Centre of Design and Architecture in Glasgow) in order to make a short film about architecture in Glasgow. An art worker showed the children round the Lighthouse and encouraged them to explore the materials used to construct the building, the design features and to contrast the old parts of the building with the new. The children appeared very comfortable in this unfamiliar space and asked lots of questions. Back in the workshop space the children had to write a script, e.g. the first clip being L is for Lighthouse and the second clip being a description of the Lighthouse. Nyrena and Asima, two Iranian girls, worked together in Farsi, their first language, and produced a description which they then explained in English to the art worker: 'The Lighthouse has a tall tower. From the outside it looks like a lighthouse by the sea'.
                    (Lady Jane Grey Field Notes, 6 May, 2003)

A young Iranian woman, Nilofar, comes to Lady Jane Grey Primary once a week and talks to the Farsi speaking children in their first language, but interacts with all the children. The Primary 6/7 children in the bilingual base were writing a piece entitled My Life for the Save the Children website. One of the Iranian pupils had written: 'I am an eleven-year-old girl and I come form Iran. I miss the sun and the wonderful cakes which my dad got me every night'.

Nilofar read what had been written and agreed with the child that she really misses Iranian cakes. A long conversation ensued in Farsi between

Nilofar and the Farsi speaking pupils in the class about their favourite cakes and the shapes and colour of these.

(Lady Jane Grey Field Notes, 6 May, 2003)

This first language interaction in both these incidents acted as a powerful force for the bilingual children's cognitive, social and cultural development and gave validation to what had been written. Further, the second incident encouraged other children to write about food they missed from their country of origin. The non-teaching adults who worked with the children offered them an audience for their ideas, an audience which admired and valued their multilingualism. The involvement of non-teaching adults with specific artistic and linguistic talents of their own provided an important additional layer in the children's educational experience, helping to ensure that education was not just about becoming enmeshed in school practices but had a role in the development of the children as bilingual learners, translators and multilingual beings.

Many of the teachers in Lady Jane Grey, like Dawn quoted above, believed firmly in making learning meaningful by taking up issues and enquiries initially introduced by the children.

> You have to be interested in and excited in what they're excited about. That is being creative. I've got to be adaptable. I've got to get in there and pitch it at their level and try and run with their interests. And I think you have to ... know the interest of the class. And I think being creative is being able to pick up on these links regardless of whether it's of my interest.   (Annette, Primary 7 class teacher)

Starting with the child's knowledge and interests often led to the children going beyond the original enquiries and surprising the teachers. The Primary 6 mainstream class were doing an Environmental Studies topic about Scotland. One of the pre-planned tasks was to write a tourist brochure about Scotland. Many of the children in the class had recently arrived in Scotland and expressed their concern to the teacher that they had never been tourists in Scotland so didn't know what to write. As a result, the children planned a day trip to Loch Lomond, a beauty spot in Scotland, not far from Glasgow, raising the money by making and selling cakes and biscuits and making all the arrangements for the travel and visit themselves.

I can't even put down what we got out of it though, it was so much ...
and the kids went through loads of different stages, there was excitement,
there was getting out of school, there was a journey, there was singing
the Loch Lomond song all the way from Glasgow to Loch Lomond ...
then there was their wee faces when they got there and when they were
on top of the tower looking across Loch Lomond. Loch Lomond made
sense and they really started to pick up on my ranting about conservation.
Now they understand why it's important to keep it beautiful and I think
they just have to see and touch.   (Jackie, Primary 6 class teacher)

Yet again, the teacher has provided the initial stimulus, but it is the children
who decided how and what they would learn from this. The teacher has been
caught up in the children's learning and liberated from the constraints of the
curriculum by the children's ability to create their own learning situations.

The children in this research, perhaps more than in other contexts, needed
to make connections between what was happening in school and what was
happening at home. Without discussing the traumatic experiences, which had
led to the children from asylum seeking families being pupils at Lady Jane
Grey Primary, suffice it to say that for the majority of children the educational
experience here was significantly different to what they or their parents had
known before. There were frequent occasions when the children demonstrated an
ability to recreate skills and knowledge learned in school into the home context,
thus increasing the relevance for them of their learning and giving them increased
ownership of the learning. They talked about how they had showed their parents
what they had been doing in school and tried out new art techniques, science
experiments and forms of writing at home, bringing the results of their labours
into the classroom. This in turn gave the children public acknowledgement of
the effort they were putting into making learning relevant to them.

There were also many incidences of the children helping the teachers to make
connections with their existing knowledge.

Jane shared the story Lima's Red Hot Chilli with the children. After the
story the children discussed some of the foodstuffs in the story, including
coconut. A Somali girl told the class that the inside of the coconut is
'hoomba'. A boy from Zimbabwe said, 'In my country there are small
coconuts.' A girl told a story of an accident trying to open a coconut. A
boy talked about the holes on top of the coconut and a girl compared

this to a bowling ball. A boy whose first language is French talked to me about something 'crée' from coconut and you mix it with something and put it in your hair like gel.

A girl commented that spaghetti looks like string or worms and a boy demonstrated how you eat spaghetti: 'You go like that: shloop.' An Iranian girl said that spaghetti in her country is called macaroni which prompted other children to talk about the names they have for pasta.

In a follow on language development activity, the children had to write sentences in a similar structure to that used in the text, e.g. 'The hairy coconut was too hard.' A boy asked 'Can you say food of your own country?' A girl wrote 'The horishzabsi was too green and a boy said 'It must be s not z. We don't say zabsi but sabsi'. Jane talked about how spelling may change when you try to transliterate from different languages, in this case Farsi. The boy said 'It's meant to be a ch sound at the beginning so I'll write it khorishtsabsee'.

(Lady Jane Grey Field Notes, 3 June, 2003)

During this activity the bilingual children were working out how to write their own language in English phonetics. The creative learning was enabled by an ethos which encouraged experimentation and home-school links. Jane commented to me after the lesson that she had thought of bringing in a coconut to help the children understand the story but it was obvious they didn't need that but may have needed a can of spaghetti. The children were again being enabled to be multilingual participants in their own learning.

Establishing relevance through teaching in the margins

Woods et al. (1999) discuss how *Teaching in the Margins* enables creative learning to take place. The naming of this concept of taking every opportunity to develop learning excited the teachers at Lady Jane Grey, who felt it validated much of what they did which could otherwise be viewed as 'just chatting'.

After lunch, the Primary 7 class were going on a visit to the local community library. While she was waiting for everyone to return from lunch, the teacher, Annette, discussed the children's favourite books. A number of children mentioned Jacqueline Wilson. Annette then referred to TV and film adaptations and asked if the children knew if Jacqueline

Wilson wrote her own adaptations and which they preferred: book or screenplay.

The children said that they preferred the book as lots is missed out in the film. Annette asked if they were disappointed in the film and a girl restated that a lot is missed out in films, offering for example, *Harry Potter* and the *Lord of the Rings*. Another girl said she had imagined characters and places and then the film was different.

A boy said he was disappointed in *The Lord of the Rings* because the book leaves you hanging and wanting to read the next book, which the film didn't. He suggested that *The Hobbit* should have been made first as a film to help people understand the story.

(Lady Jane Grey Field Notes, 12 June, 2003)

Annette could have used this time for administration but chose instead to discuss books and films, giving value to the children's experiences. Natasha referred to this constant teaching when she discussed her enjoyment of the job in the bilingual base.

I think more people should have experience of this (teaching bilingual children). It really makes you aware of what you're doing; why you're doing it. You have to really question yourself all the time: Why am I doing this? What are they getting from it? I enjoy it. I get a real thrill from it. I think it's really challenging and I love the push that it gives me. I love the fact that I do have to work really hard. I know that sounds really pathetic but I do. ... I'm not just following textbooks or prescribed texts. I like the fact that I have to think about it all.

(Natasha, Primary 2/3 Bilingual base teacher)

The teachers at Lady Jane Grey Primary identified constant teaching and flexibility as central to their practice. These factors helped them to spontaneously respond to learners' interests, another feature which Woods et al. (1999) consider enables creative teaching.

Teaching Strategies

Further consideration and identification of teacher strategies and perspectives for developing creative learning in Lady Jane Grey Primary indicated a number of issues concerning school and classroom organisation that led to pupils to learning creatively.

Space is used imaginatively by the teachers. Although the school is a traditional Victorian building with separate classroom spaces, furnished with tables and chairs, the teachers carefully consider the best use of space for the teaching that is planned. The existence of some empty spaces in the school due to falling roles has enhanced the ability for a creative use of the space. On arriving in any particular classroom area it is not always predictable what it will look like, so all furniture may have been moved to the sides of the room to create a large open floor space for role play; a spare room may have clothes racks, trunks of clothes and curtained areas to provide a backstage changing room for a performance; the furniture and instruments may have been removed from the music room to create space for the children to experiment with the boxes of 'junk' (paper, tins, tubes, dried beans, and wire) to make their own instruments; or the head teacher's office may have been kitted out with video recording equipment to enable the children to conduct interviews with members of staff. Or indeed, the activities for the session may not be within the confines of the school walls but, rather, in the local playground, park, library, supermarket or recycling centre.

A significant feature of the teaching developed by Jane, the team leader of the bilingual base is collaborative teaching. Jane focuses on collaboration between pupils as essential for the achievement of the bilingual learners, but also on collaboration between teachers as being essential for this achievement. Collaboration is a teaching and learning strategy that is worked towards for the mutual benefit of children, parents, staff and wider community.

> So there might be children who are creatively thinking but it might be in their own language and without putting them in situations where you want them to work together collaboratively and use either their own language or English or a mixture of both then you don't get that creative thinking or collaborative working. (Jane, Primary 6/7 bilingual base teacher and team leader)

She strives to achieve collaboration between teachers by working hard for the whole school as well as for the base. She acknowledges that this collaborative teaching is a difficult ethos to establish in a situation where people have been used to teaching their own class and discusses the steps she took to develop this:

There's a lot of judgements and I felt as if I had to come in (to the school) and prove myself (to the teachers) so the first few months I took classes and lead the lesson. Now I'm trying to get them more involved as well. So that's the stage I'm at just now. I think we're getting there.

(Jane Primary 6/7 bilingual base teacher and team leader)

Jane recognises that the organisation and indeed existence of the base could mitigate the collaboration between mainstream and asylum seeking children and for this reason, she believes the extra-curricular clubs provide an essential space for co-participation:

It's good that there's a mixture of kids there as well. I like the kids all being together and mixing, even the mixture of ages 'cos it's Primary 4-Primary 7(eight to twelve-year-old children). I think it's also good for the bilingual kids who are with me a lot of the time because I'm aware how often they're with me 'cos it's maths and language in the morning and reception in the afternoon so they're really only in class for an hour a day... so it's not a lot of time in the (mainstream) class and I think that also contributes to the fact that they don't say much (in the mainstream) cos they're not in enough to make the bonds with the other kids ...

She considers that sometimes the practice of the mainstream class however may not promote collaboration:

and they are all working separately ... and it is a shame that we don't have more English as an Additional Language staff where we could go into the class but then that would just cause other problems 'cos you're working silently and you can't really play your language game in big loud voices or ... or sit on the floor.

While clearly being in favour of independent thinking and creative learning, Jane considers that as a teacher you operate in a way which does not in fact promote creativity, and that it can be beneficial for children to work with other adults who will not try to take control of their ideas:

I think as teachers you do get very bogged down in being the font of all knowledge, so thinking the children will not be able to do that unless I show them or tell them how to do it and I think sometimes as a teacher you don't give them freedom ...

Referring to the Art Club visits to The Lighthouse, Jane acknowledged some initial scepticism as to the children's ability to do what was required:

... I mean even when they (the children) were doing their own ideas I was still going round sticking my oar in, is that the one you're choosing? Oh that's not a very good one really, is it? and before you know it I've told them what to do instead of they had chosen something completely different. It's trying to step back but other adults, who are not teachers, do that (step back) more and just give them the freedom. So it's really good that they're getting the chance to mix with adult adults, as opposed to teacher adults, real adults.

Collaborating with other adults and professionals is one of the benchmarks which are used to indicate if student teachers in Scotland are ready to graduate as probationer teachers. Student teachers are given targeted opportunities to undertake collaborative activities but are also expected to develop the skills of collaboration as they study, record the collaborative ventures they have been engaged in and reflect on the outcomes of these. However, the nature of many primary schools in Scotland means that the opportunities for real collaboration are limited with teachers mainly having individual responsibility and autonomy for their own class. Jane, and indeed the other three GASSP teachers under her leadership, are striving to achieve collaboration in the school and raised some of the difficulties they encountered. However, the collaboration in this school was frequently characterised by relationships outside the classroom.

At the time of the visit to The Lighthouse, Jane would have normally had teaching responsibility for the Primary 6 and 7 reception group.

The children from the reception group who are not in the art club will be in their mainstream classes this afternoon and Jane tells them what work they can do if they are not involved in the class work.
(Lady Jane Grey Field Notes).

This arrangement is indicative of good cooperation between staff. Although the class teachers did not expect to have the reception children in their class that afternoon there was no expression of resentment. The children did not show concern at a change to their routine, indicative of their feeling of security within the school. They were happy to be in the bilingual base for reception or to be in the mainstream class. None of the children who were not going on the trip to the Lighthouse express envy towards the children who were going. The children all have their own choice of after school activity and this often involves participation in out of school events.

Talk in the staff room was characterised by the ways in which the teachers interacted and listened to and cared about each other. There were no apparent cliques and everyone seemed interested in everyone else. Many topics of conversation were covered in the break times but, although there were usually about twelve staff in the room, when one person spoke, everyone listened. There was a general air that what anyone said was important and interesting. Many of the teachers share out of school pursuits. They talk to the children about these as well as to the other teachers. The refugee children are not seen as the concern only of the base but of the whole school and genuine sympathy was expressed for the racism experienced by children who have already faced many traumas prior to arriving in Glasgow. Shared experiences among some members of staff become vicarious experiences for the whole staff. The teachers also shared their out of school experiences, via photos and stories, with the children they teach who could see at first hand that the teachers had a life outside school and were friendly with each other.

This respect for, and interest in, others' feelings and opinions, is carried into the classrooms and reflected in the relationships between teachers and pupils.

The teachers themselves place a high value on their own learning, engaging in numerous in-service activities and reporting on these to colleagues and discussing how they will take what they have learned into the classroom.

Although there is considerable team teaching in the school, largely as a result of the bilingual base teachers working alongside their mainstream colleagues to facilitate the mainstreaming of the bilingual children, this team teaching is not always characterised by collaboration. In the Primary 7 class there are two job-sharing teachers. There is genuine collaboration when Jane and Annette team teach, marked, for example, by them finishing off each others' sentences and looking to each other for what to do next. This collaboration is something which Jane is striving to develop and has not yet been achieved to the same extent with the other class teacher, although by sitting watching and listening and responding to pupil needs, she also indicates she is on the way to collaboration.

Annette commented in an interview on the team teaching and its benefits for the bilingual pupils:

> We have to integrate an awful lot more so they (the bilingual pupils) do not see Jane being their teacher 'cos we do things together.
>
> (Annette, Primary 7 mainstream teacher)

The bilingual base teachers discussed the constraints of full collaboration further, in response to a starter paper from myself and commented,

This collaboration (as described above for Jane and Annette) is not always possible. Constraints such as planning time together sometimes means it's easier to split the class in half and each take a mixed group (bilingual and monolingual). This ensures that the bilingual children are integrated into the mainstream class, but the smaller number makes it more manageable. The perfect situation would be to have a mixture of this with other lessons being team taught. Unfortunately, this is not always possible for many reasons.

The bilingual base teachers and some of the mainstream teachers frequently choose, when discussing their teaching, to use a discourse which, according to Woods (1990) can be characterised as creativity based. That is, it involved features of relevance, control, ownership, innovation. Thus, Dawn, the Primary teacher quoted earlier in this paper, used relevance as a key term in discussing how her teaching differs now from when she was a mainstream class teacher. I asked Dawn if her experience teaching the children from asylum seeking families would have an impact on her teaching in the mainstream.

> Oh, definitely, ... every lesson, it's just amazing the difference you get out the children. I mean the rewards you get and the work you get back if you put the input in is tremendous, but you've got to have the props, you've got to cart everything in from home, you know, and, and make it real for them, so I'd definitely change my ways.
>
> (Dawn, Primary 1 Bilingual Base Teacher).

The base and the children have also affected the mainstream teachers' approach to teaching and some of these teachers are also using the discourse of creative teaching. Here, Annette talks passionately about the need to make the teaching relevant to the children even if the content is not something in which she is interested. She wants the children to take control of their learning by contributing their ideas and interests and believes that her role is to be flexible and responsive so that the children will have ownership of the knowledge:

> The kids are bringing in ideas and I love the kids bringing books to me. I hate *Lord of the Rings*; I hate it with a passion; I can't abide it. But I now know all the characters and I go back and I have to slog my way through these things 'cos it's the interest of the children ... you've got to be adaptable. I have to get in there, pitch it at their level, and try to run with their interests. And ... each year I don't come to it thinking I can do the same as I did before. I cannot, you just cannot, you do not know the dynamics of the class; you do not know the interest of the class. And I think being creative is being able to pick up on these links and regardless of whether it's of my interest;... But I think you always have to be prepared to go with something ... you have to be able to draw the links. I think you have to be really ready to adapt. And I have to watch Big Brother (a popular television programme). I have to be aware of what's going on. You have to know the lingo (vernacular). You have to or you're becoming passive. You're not pitching it at the level for them. ... I have to be down at that level and know what fun is and keep up. That is being creative. You have to be interested in and excited in what they're excited about.
>
> (Annette, Primary 7 mainstream teacher)

Jackie, the Primary 6 mainstream teacher, is excited about the way in which the bilingual children in her class have made her re-evaluate her teaching style:

> I think it's really positive, ... although it can be hard work, and sometimes it's a bit... daunting when you realise that a child's really not understanding what I'm saying at the moment, how am I going to communicate this in a different way, and that's when I realise I'm the queen of hand movements, and that on some occasions I just look like a windmill, for (I'm) constantly moving my hands, but the other day the kids and I were talking about the ground and I said 'mossy' and they all made this movement before I did and they've started picking it up. Mossy was scooting little fingers together, I just thought that was fab, that sums up how the teaching in the room's going now, we're all doing it
>
> (Jackie, Primary 6 mainstream teacher).

Jackie has acknowledged that the children are important in the teaching process as well as her. She contrasts her teaching now with how she used to teach six years ago and recalls fondly the creative teaching that she received as a child.

> When I was at college they were talking about *5 to 14* (the Scottish curriculum guidelines), and I was a great believer in *5 to 14* curriculum because it offers us structure, and progression and yes, you need structure, you can't just go willy-nilly and go and teach something and have no structure, you must have it planned. When you're a new teacher you need structure and you need to follow steps. I used to listen to some of the older teachers, my mother and aunts included, and go 'No, you need to have something to follow, you need a guideline, you need a book' and now I've been teaching for six years and I want to go back to the way my mum and aunt talk about teaching, and about the teaching that I remember getting at school. We started an art project on animals, it then became a topic, as a class we made a ten foot *papier-mâché* shark, which I believe still hangs in the foyer of my old primary school. I remember giving up lunchtimes to make the *papier-mâché* shark, and on reflection the teacher must have been straight out of college, very enthusiastic and he must have cursed that shark for six months of his life because he was there doing it every lunch time. I just think that it's now too focused on academics. There's no spontaneity, there is no 'right, we were talking about biscuits, let's make biscuits this afternoon', we can't, we're doing something else, and it's working out how we can justify on paper what teachers my mothers age have been saying for fifteen years, and now I'm starting to realise that, yeah, they were right.
>
> (Jackie, Primary 6 mainstream teacher)

Throughout this interview Jackie used the discourse of creative teaching and learning. She seems to consider creative teaching to be a more mature form of teaching than the restrictive curriculum centred teaching which currently dominates Scottish education.

In addition to teaching strategies such as the use of space and team teaching and the use of a creative teaching discourse in the school, the teachers, both in the bilingual base and in the mainstream classrooms, make use of learner inclusive/co-participative pedagogies which enhance the children's ability to take ownership and control of their learning.

Although the classes are initially organised on an age-related basis there were frequent opportunities for cross-age co-participation. Older children read their stories to younger children; younger children shared their findings with older children; and mixed age groups went together on excursions into the community to investigate features such as recycling, play facilities and urban wildlife.

Children were encouraged to use all their linguistic resources to enable learning to take place. Inter and intra-language collaboration enhanced understanding as children helped newcomers to participate by repeating the task requirements in another language.

Teachers were responsive to learner suggestions for development as the Primary 6 teacher, mentioned earlier in this paper, who while undertaking an Environmental Studies topic on Scotland realised that the children had little experience of Scotland beyond the high rise flats. The teacher talked expansively about the value of the children's experience of organising and undertaking the trip to Loch Lomond discussed earlier in the chapter for learning across the curriculum, despite the activity being out with the original plans:

> I had to ditch my official timetable, but we did writing, because we talked about making the biscuits, we did measuring because we measured the ingredients, we did everything that we needed to cover in the curriculum, but it's very hard to prove. We were restless and we were tired and it's been a long winter and we needed fresh air -- when you're surrounded by high rises all day long, sometimes you need to go and look at a green mountain, and really the basis of the trip was to run around the wilderness and that's kind of it.   (Jackie, Primary 6 mainstream teacher)

In addition to these pedagogies the school, largely since the arrival of the bilingual base, involved adults other than teachers in the children's education. Parents made costumes for school performances and made a mosaic to display in the school showing the languages of the school. The janitor and classroom assistants showed the children games they used to play in the playground. Volunteers from the community used their first language in the classrooms to communicate with children new to English. The involvement of outside experts such as art workers, the use of the local environment and the importance of after school 'clubs' have already been highlighted as further examples of inclusive and co-participative pedagogies employed by the school.

The change in pedagogy which has resulted from the arrival of the bilingual pupils has enabled the mainstream teachers to be liberated from the constraints of the curriculum and performativity demands. This could not have happened without the support of local, i.e. school level management, and this has indeed been a feature of the developing creative pedagogy in the school. The co-participation of children, bilingual base teachers, mainstream teachers, management, non-teaching staff and other adults in the school and wider community has led to a situation where newly arrived bilingual children are using all their linguistic and cultural resources to take control of their learning. A highly effective creative learning environment has evolved which has impacted positively not only on the children and their perception of education in Scotland, but has also led the teachers to re-evaluate their role in the learning process.

Lady Jane Grey Primary as a multilingual conference

To date, I have reflected on how the features of creative teaching identified by Woods et al. manifested themselves in Lady Jane Grey Primary. What Woods et al. (1999) did not discuss however, was collaboration as a characteristic of creative teaching and learning.

In this research site, collaboration between the children was essential, particularly due to the limited English of fifty percent of the pupils. The teachers used pedagogies such as cross-age co-participation and inter and intra-language collaboration to assist the children to be creative learners and also to enable integration of the children from asylum-seeking families. In addition to this, the teachers worked and played together, modelling teamwork and co-operation in their daily routines, although they do not suggest that this was easy.

A monolingual school in an economically deprived area of an inner city can become an effective multilingual, multiracial school, which gives an enhanced place to the perspectives of all its pupils, while ensuring that the children from asylum seeking families are able to make meaning of and become active members of the school community. However, new policies In this area need to be based on the needs of the children from asylum seeking families and endorsed and supported by the school management, the teachers and the non-teaching staff.

There is at work a multilingual conference where the pupils work both as participants, presenters and simultaneous translators. The teachers in the school provide the stimulus for the children's development of their own learning, acting in this multilingual conference as highly effective keynote speakers. Other adults in the school and wider community are the audience essential to the children's belief in them as participants and presenters. A complication to this metaphor, which enhances the role played by the children in the conference, is that the children themselves frequently take over the microphone from the keynote speakers, deciding on what is relevant and how it will be developed.

References

Bentley, T. (2001) The Creative Society: Reuniting Schools and Lifelong Learning in Fielding, M. (ed.) *Taking Education really Seriously: Four Years' Hard Labour*, London: Routledge Falmer

Bourne, J. (1990) Local Authority Provision for bilingual pupils *Educational Research* 32(1): 3-13

Bourne, J. (1997) The Continuing Revolution: Teaching as Learning in the Mainstream Multilingual Classroom in Leung, C. and Cable, C. (eds) *English as an Additional language: Changing Perspectives*, Watford: NALDIC

Bruce, T. (1991) *Time to Play in Early Childhood Education*, Sevenoaks: Hodder and Stoughton

Cummins, J. (1977) Cognitive Factors associated with the attainment of intermediate levels of bilingual skills, *Modern Language Journal*, 61: 3-12

Cummins, J. (1996) *Negotiating Identities: Education for Empowerment in a Diverse Society*, Ontario: California Association for Bilingual Education

Department of Education and Science (DES) (1963) *English for Immigrants*, London: DES

Department of Education and Science (DES) (1975) *A Language for Life: The Bullock Report*, London: HMSO

Department of Education and Science (DES) (1985) *Education for All: The Swann Report*, London: HMSO

Department of Education and Science (DES) (1989) *English for Ages 5-16: The Cox Report*, London: HMSO

Department of Education and Science (DES) (1990) *Modern Foreign Languages for Ages 11-16: The Harris Report*, London: HMSO

Glasgow Asylum Seekers' Support Project (GASSP) Education Handbook (2001), Glasgow, Glasgow City Council Education Services

Herriman, M. and Burnaby, B. (1996) *Language Policies in English-Dominant Countries*, Clevedon: Multilingual Matters

Lambert, W.E. (1980) The social Psychology of Language in Giles et al. (eds.) *Language: Social Psychological Perspectives*, Oxford: Pergamon

Lauren, U. (1991) A creativity index for studying the free written production for bilinguals *International Journal of Applied Linguistics*, 1(2): 198-208

Meek, M. (1985) Play and paradoxes: Some considerations of Imagination and Language in Wells, G. and Nicholls, J. (eds) *Language and Learning: an Interactional Perspective*, London: Falmer Press

Mills, R.W and Mills, J. (1993) *Bilingualism in the Primary School*, London: Routledge

Moyles, J. (1989) *Just Playing? The role and status of play in early childhood education,* Buckingham: Open University Press

Ricciardelli, L.A. (1992) Creativity and bilingualism, *Journal of Creative Behaviour,* 26(4): 242-254

Scottish Consultative Council On The Curriculum (SCCC) (1994) *Languages for Life,* Dundee SCCC

Smyth, G. (2001) 'I feel this challenge—but I don't have the background': Teachers' responses to their bilingual pupils in 6 Scottish primary schools: an ethnographic study Open University, unpublished Ph.D. thesis

Stubbs, M (1994) Educational Language Planning in England and Wales: Multicultural Rhetoric and Assimilationist Assumptions, in Maybin, J. (ed.): *Language and Literacy in Social Practice,* Clevedon: Multilingual Matters

Thompson, L., Fleming, M., and Byram, M. (1996) 'Languages and Language Policy in Britain' in Herriman, M. and Burnaby, B., *Language Policies in English-Dominant Countries,* Clevedon: Multilingual Matters

Wiles, S. (1985) Language and Learning in Multi-Ethnic Classrooms: Strategies for Supporting Bilingual Students in Wells, G. and Nicholls, J. *Language and Learning: an Interactional Perspective,* London: Falmer Press

Woodhead, C. (1995) *Chief Inspector's Annual Report,* London: OFSTED

Woods, P. (1990) *Teacher Skills and Strategies* London: Falmer

Woods, P., Boyle, M. and Hubbard, N. (1999) *Multicultural Children in the Early Years,* Clevedon: Multilingual Matters.

Woods, P. and Jeffrey, B. (1996) *Teachable Moments: The Art Of Creative Teaching In Primary Schools,* Buckingham: Open University Press

Structure and agency in the construction of creative teaching and learning: A view from the margins

Ciaran Sugrue
St. Patrick's College, Dublin City University

Introduction

As change forces wreak their 'vengeance' (Fullan, 2003) on the internal workings of schools and classrooms; while policy makers intensify their efforts to improve standards and global competitiveness decrees that all systems, particularly those in the developed world, must maintain if not enhance their market share in the borderless market schools must play their part in ensuring that all who pass through their portals be equipped to contribute to the 'knowledge economy' (Hargreaves, 2003). In the relentless pursuit of improving test scores, there is increasing homogenisation of schooling and what counts as 'good schools'. As Cuban suggests

> In the twenty-first century, business leaders, educators, and public officials no longer define the bottom line as better teaching and learning; the bottom line is securing higher test scores. (2003).

He argues persuasively that: 'standards-based performance and accountability has weakened progressive teaching practices while hardening traditional teaching patterns (op. cit.). In such circumstances, it may seem somewhat foolhardy to undertake research on creative learning and teaching, particularly from learners' perspectives, since top-down coercive policy agendas have reduced their role to passive fodder for Standard Assessment Tasks and their equivalent in other jurisdictions.

Labaree, summing up the current state of play in the U.S.A context states

> Instruction in American schools is overwhelmingly teacher-centred; classroom management is the teacher's top priority; traditional school subjects dominate the curriculum; textbooks and teacher talk are the primary means of delivering this curriculum; learning consists of recalling what texts and teachers say; tests measure how much of this students have

learned; and the tests drive the classroom process. In short, traditional
methods of teaching and learning are in control.   (2004)

Against a pervasive coercive rhetoric of 'one best school', it may be argued that
research on creative teaching and learning is very timely as well as being vitally
necessary. Greater 'ingenuity' (Homer-Dixon, 2001), imagination and creativity
are needed more than ever to deal with the challenges, not only posed by the
knowledge economy, but also by the knowledge society (Hargreaves, 2003).

This paper sets out to capture some of the more salient aspects of creative
teaching and learning amidst this maelstrom of reform. It is in five parts. First,
we provide a brief account of the Irish policy context and traditions of teaching
within primary schooling. Second, we outline the nature of the study that led
to the generation of data used in this paper and its methodological approach.
Third, we articulate some theoretical perspectives as a means of providing both
a backdrop to subsequent analysis and as a lens through which to analyse data.
Fourth, we identify prominent aspects of the agency of teachers and learners,
with particular emphasis on the latter, by adopting a grounded theory approach
and staying close to the data. Three major 'themes' are described and illustrated
under the more general framework derived from the data of 'spaces for learning'.
There will be greater emphasis throughout this section on the agency of the
individual participants, while indicating also the constraining influences of
context, location and the structure of relations. Fifth, we draw some tentative
conclusions regarding creative teaching and learning, while indicating also, where
future analysis of data may need to thread.

Irish policy context and traditions of teaching

It is generally accepted that Irish society has changed radically and rapidly
during the past two decades (Sugrue, 2004; Corcoran and Peillon, 2002; O'
Connell, 2001). The decade of the 1990s in particular, while playing host to
unprecedented economic growth, and feted as the 'Celtic Tiger economy', also
bore witness to a raft of legislation on education, welfare, child-care, equality
and disability, all of which impinge significantly on educational provision, while
there was simultaneously a veritable continuous cascade of education reports
and policy papers. From a primary schooling perspective, probably the high
water mark of reform initiatives was the launching of the 'revised' primary
school curriculum in September of 1999 (Government of Ireland, 1999). In
the intervening years, the government implemented a national programme

of professional development for teachers through the Primary Curriculum Support Programme (PCSP), through the secondment of several primary principals and teachers from their regular positions to facilitate courses on the revised curriculum. This initiative typically resulted in six days per annum being provided to all teachers, four of which were out of school, with the other two days being in school for planning purposes as follow up to the out of school provision. So intensive did this become, that principals in particular sought respite to allow some time to absorb reforms into school routines. The government suspended the programme for a year, but since September of 2004, the roll out of reform has recommenced. This initiative was also accompanied by a similarly orchestrated reform initiative—School Development Planning Programme (SDPS). From a position therefore, a few short years ago, where professional learning was individual and idiosyncratic, professional support, from the perspective of practitioners, was beginning to feel more like an additional burden rather than something genuinely educative. The revised curriculum places greater emphasis on objectives, specified learning outcomes, with a strong emphasis on constructivism and differentiation (Government of Ireland, 1999). During the summer of 2004, the Minister for Education and Science announced the introduction of national testing for primary schooling at two points in the primary cycle to commence in 2007. Many of these developments, and national testing in particular, are consistent with international trends and a generally homogenising tendency due to globalisation.

Traditions of schooling in Ireland are generally recognised to be conservative, and rooted in tradition despite recent reform efforts and the international conformist tendency towards homogenisation wrought by global forces, For example, a visiting committee of the OECD commented in 1991 that:

> To understand contemporary Ireland, it is necessary to recognise how much its remote as well as more recent history still affects public values and attitudes and offers a key to understanding its institutions, not least its system of education. (OECD, 1991).

Nevertheless, while there is an obvious need to pay attention to issues of continuity as well as shifting perspectives the extent of change in the past decade should not be underestimated. O' Connell, in his appropriately titled book, *Changed Utterly*, suggests that:

Perhaps ... we have been racing from what we were towards what we are now without much reflection or planning in between—a change based on panic and self-disgust.   (2001)

He concludes that without serious and sustained efforts to look at ourselves in the mirror, we are more likely to 'experience change, but without transformation'. This important health warning is timely also in the education field. Despite attempts in 1971 to introduce radical education change through the introduction of a child-centred curriculum, subsequent research evidence, suggests that teachers adopted the rhetoric of progressivism, while teaching routines continued to be largely traditional and teacher centred (see Sugrue, 1997). A deeply conservative, essentialist and anti-intellectual thinking pervaded Irish psyche and society until recently (see Lynch and Lodge, 2002; O' Connell, 2001; Lee, 1989; Fitzgerald, 1991); one in which control of the imagination rather than the cultivation of creativity was frequently a major preoccupation. A consequence of this is that imagination and creativity are words used sparingly (if at all) among the teaching profession discussing issues of practice. It is much more common to hear the more neutral, if more nebulous term, of 'good' teaching or the accolade of 'good' teacher applied to individual members of the profession. More occasionally, if the term 'creative' (or talented) is attributed to a teacher, it is most likely that this is understood as being 'blessed' with a personal talent in Art or Music, that such an individual has 'flair', but it is understood as a 'gift', rather than the consequence of application and hard work. Consequently, there is no attendant onus on others, perhaps less talented, gifted or creative, to work towards developing such skills and expertise. Being creative and imaginative appears divined by the god of the genome or social circumstances, a kind of fatalism that sees such personal characteristics as predetermined by the lottery of life. Consequently, there is no necessity to develop more generalised notions of creativity. This may be a legacy or continuity within traditions of teaching and cultures of schooling in the setting, while it is also likely that teachers' identities, their own biographies, and social location, play a role (see Sugrue, 1996). These important contextual factors have significance for the study of creative teaching and learning in the setting and we discuss them later in section three which focuses on theoretical perspectives on creativity. First, however, it is necessary to focus attention on methodological considerations in the conduct of the research.

Methodological considerations and participants

There were three sites for this ethnographic study of creative teaching and learning from learners' perspectives. The participants were primary teachers, two female, and one male. The data analysed in this paper is from one site only, where there was prolonged engagement. Data generation took place on a regular basis throughout the school year 2003-4. While data analysis has been an ongoing part of the study from the outset, more systematic and in-depth analysis commenced during the summer of 2004 and is ongoing. This, chapter therefore, may be read as an initial attempt to map aspects of creative teaching in this particular site.

Strumpet City (pseudonym) is the school context in which Tony, a veteran teacher with more than twenty years teaching experience, works in a 'special class', consisting of six learners, all boys, as well as a teaching assistant, a mature woman. The school is officially designated as disadvantaged and was established in the mid 1960s, and, as the following extract from the first set of field notes indicates, after an initial period of rapid expansion, the school has now settled down to a more stable pupil number.

> The school now has its third principal since its foundation. The school has now settled down to a more 'stable' population of four hundred pupils with a compliment of twenty-six teachers after an initial period of rapid expansion in the early 1970s when the school population in the boy's school exceeded 1,100 and there were thirty-one teachers. The staff now constitutes principal, deputy, eighteen male, and eight female teachers, with three learning support teachers, two special class teachers, one resource, one giving children an even break and one home school community liaison teacher. The school is unusual in the relatively high compliment of male teachers, when the national figure is approximately eighty per cent female and twenty per cent male, while an increasing number of schools have no male teachers. (Field Notes)

The various 'additional' teachers listed above are indicative of a series of government initiatives to tackle disadvantage. Tony is one of the two special class teachers and a regular feature of the school day is for the senior class, for which he has responsibility, to adjourn each morning to the junior special class where all partake of 'breakfast', consisting of hot tea and toasted sandwiches. For many of the learners this is their first 'meal' of the day. Tony began his teaching career in this school, first as a regular classroom teacher, and later, having completed further study in Special Needs education, he has been responsible for special classes for a number of years. More recently, he has completed a Masters in Education and his specialisation and area of interest within this programme was ICT. Not surprisingly therefore, communications technologies feature strongly in his classroom, and they are a very definite part of his pedagogy.

I was in the privileged position of being able to get to know these learners particularly well as a researcher during the study due to the fact that there were only six learners only in this classroom, For this reason, analysis in this paper includes important elements of life history in tandem with and complementary to more traditional ethnographic fieldwork. Seeking to document creative teaching and learning from learners' perspectives in particular, can be strengthened significantly in my view by including aspects of life story and life history since the latter is 'interested in the way people *do* narrate their lives, not in the way they should' (Goodson and Sikes, 2001). A chapter that also seeks to indicate the structural constraints on creative teaching and learning, as well as indicate the agency of teacher and learners, needs to pay particular attention to context. By 'providing contextual data, life stories can be seen in the light of changing patterns of time and space in testimony and action as social constructions' (Goodson and Sikes, 2001). From the point of view of crafting as comprehensive an account of the nature of teaching and learning in Strumpet City therefore, I draw on elements of life story, while seeking to construct partial life histories of the actors, in an attempt to provide a more grounded and contextualised account. Collectively, they became known affectionately to me in the field notes (for contextual reasons that are confidential) as 'the gang', inspired to some extent by the title of Peter Carey's book, *True History of the Kelly Gang* (2000). The gang members include—Ben, Dan, Duncan, Jim, Kenny and Kevin (all pseudonyms) and some more others came from difficult and dysfunctional family circumstances, thus leaving them vulnerable as well as requiring delicate handling almost all of the time.

Tony's classroom was frequently referred to as the 'unit' but 'gang' seems more appropriate to a 'band' of learners thrown together by a confluence of circumstances. I do not want to paint them as victims; they would not thank me for it. Humour and spontaneity punctuated their day since they shared the same interests as their peers. They typically spent the morning in the 'unit' while later in the day they joined a mainstream class for various subjects. Consequently, navigating between the mainstream and the margins emerges in analysis as an important constraint on their learning and identities, their teacher's and their own agency. An important member of the 'gang' also is Margaret, a mature woman, employed as a Special Needs Assistant (SNA) to work with Kevin but she was an invaluable resource to everyone in the room and her care and interest in their general well-being as well as their learning was exemplary. At first glance, the 'unit' may not strike the reader as the most fertile ground for creative teaching and learning. Even if this is your mindset, I think that the analysis below will change your mind. Data were analysed using the constant comparative method, and the general approach adopted was grounded theory.

Theoretical Perspectives

For the purpose of this project, apart from a general commitment to ethnography, I also took seriously, Woods' paraphrasing of what Best (1991) wrote about creativity when he says:

> Best recommends what he calls the 'Personal Enquiry' approach, which involves developing qualities such as 'curiosity, originality, initiative, cooperation, perseverance, open-mindedness, self-criticism, responsibility, self-confidence and independence (1991). This is what makes a creative individual, imbued with the spirit of creative enquiry.
>
> (Woods, 1996)

These comments are in sharp contrast to views expressed by me above regarding the positioning of 'creativity' within the teaching community in the Irish context. Consequently, my tendency was to avoid the use of such language while being vigilant for the kind of characteristics identified above.

My own primary school teaching experience was in similarly disadvantaged areas of greater Dublin. Consequently, I am easily convinced of the 'emotional labour' involved in working in such contexts, and the toll it takes on some teacher's physical and mental well-being. Put more positively, since pressures for reform have intensified in recent years and where traditional authority and power relations eroded, trust has become a key and precious commodity. This is particularly the case in teaching where a positive climate of trust and risk are essential ingredients in constructing positive learning experiences (Giddens, 1991; Troman and Woods, 2001). Paying attention to the nature of relationships in researching creative teaching is a key concern. This takes on heightened significance in the classroom context explored and documented in this chapter where each individual learner is 'special' and brings to the learning situation a previous history, experiences of schooling that are often negative. In such circumstances, establishing trust becomes a major challenge to the teacher.

Apart from the often intense nature of the emotional labour involved in teaching the kind of pupils Thompson (2002) calls 'rustbelt kids', those on the margins of the global economy, she indicates also that 'time devoted to welfare and discipline is *not* demanded of all schools'. Tony, his colleagues and principal, very definitely share Thompson's view that 'a hallmark of the disadvantaged school is the time taken managing order and welfare and the resulting lack of time and resources to do as much as might be done to change curriculum, pedagogy and school practices'. Nevertheless, it is important to recognise that emotions play a powerful role in creativity. Oatley and Jenkins (1998) suggest that they are 'like a painter's palette, the bases of elaboration ... emotions are like modes of locomotion that we are innately given—creeping on all fours, walking, running, jumping—which allow for creative elaboration ...' For the members of 'the gang', for whom school has been a negative experience, and who bring turbulent life stories to the classroom door, they represent a considerable emotional challenge to Tony's ingenuity, to create a positive learning environment that is emotionally warm, secure and imaginative. Consequently, as I will argue later in the analysis, that the emotional climate, and the disposition of the teacher in such circumstances are crucial to the teaching learning situation. This perspective sits comfortably with Wood's assertion that 'excellence in teaching requires artistry ... that the teacher is able to exploit opportunities as they occur' (1996). However, here too, there is ambiguity in the use of language. Is 'excellence in teaching' co-terminus with 'creative' teaching?

In subsequent research, Woods appears to provide a positive response to this question. Creative teachers, he asserts, display four major components in their pedagogies: 'innovation, ownership, control and relevance' (1995). He also suggests that relationships, naturalism, scaffolding and balance are important element of pedagogy (op.cit.). Rather than elaborate on these ingredients at this point, it may be more profitable to locate these aspects of creative teaching and learning within the specific context under investigation and to reconstruct these elements of pedagogy from the bottom up. A major aspect of this analysis will be to bring together the disposition of the teacher, his stance towards teaching, as well as the pedagogical constructions to which this disposition gives rise. This side of the coin needs to be juxtaposed with the dispositions, perspectives and behaviours of learners.

'Spaces for learning'

During my initial visits to the school and classroom, and my uncertain conversations with the 'gang' members, I tentatively inquired as to what they liked best about this classroom. Invariably the response was 'the Sir'; their respect and admiration for Tony was apparently boundless, but this did not mean that they did not have 'their moments' with him. Rather, that they felt secure in his presence, and were in no doubt that he had their best interests at heart, and that he would be an advocate for them if such a situation warranted it. I began to call the teacher affectionately—Sir Tony!

After several visits to the classroom, the field notes began to use the term 'spaces for learning' as an over-arching notion that sought to capture the disposition of the teacher as well as describe pedagogical routines and manoeuvres. I recognised that such spaces are both physical and psychological. During the previous school year, Tony and his learners, which included three of the present group, created space for the 'mindstorms' *Lego* work, collectively they transformed an old storeroom into a workshop by painting, making a workbench and erecting shelves around the walls. The place was laden with a plethora of *Lego* kits. Tony had installed a camera in the workshop with a small monitor back in the classroom so that having built trust with a learner or learners the keys to go work in the 'shop' were given to them while he could also keep an eye on them. At other times he made it very clear that the monitor was turned off, thus increasing the trust and responsibility being invested in these learners. Trust was established and responsibility in a slow and incremental manner and gradually taken by learners as the following extract seeks to illustrate.

At this point Tony gave the keys of the 'storeroom' to Kevin with instructions to seek out the paints. Kevin clearly relished his new 'big' responsibility. One of the other boys (Kenny) decided to go along with him, and Tony turned on the video monitor/camera to keep an eye on them both as they entered the room on the floor below. The former storeroom doubles as a secure place to keep additional *Lego* materials and as a 'workshop' where individuals or a small number can work on their own, being independent, while the video link enables Tony to monitor behaviour etc. They both began to 'shift' the paints from the classroom to the workshop, while it seemed apparent that Kenny was playing a subordinate role, taking instruction from Kevin who was in charge, by dint of having been given custody of the keys. It seemed that the subtext of the ritual was not lost on the individuals concerned, and on Kevin in particular, who seemed to take on the new responsibility bestowed on him by his teacher. There are subtle roles, routines and responsibilities played out while everything has an air of informality, and thoughtfully orchestrated. They are intended to foster a climate of trust where learners are given more latitude as they respond positively to the overtures of 'the Sir' to take more responsibility by way of running the show as well as becoming 'masters' of their own learning. In a conversation with Tony later, we both speculated as to how this approach 'jived' with the experience of these learners when they joined mainstream classes at various times during the day.   (Field Notes)

From a structural perspective therefore, our conversations revealed at least a tentative awareness that positive aspects of pedagogy and learning in the confines of 'the unit' might not serve learners well as they navigated between the margins and the mainstream. The agency of learners (facilitated by their teacher) had potential also to conflict with the pedagogical structures in mainstream classes. Consequently, what was transformative in one context became a liability down the corridor. However, at this point my primary concern is to indicate the characteristics of creative teaching and learning rather than become preoccupied with structural constraints. Suffice to say that a powerful pedagogy, depending on its structural location, can be both enabling and disabling and the lines between the two are often fuzzy, moving and confusing, particularly from a learner's perspective.

There are many facets making up this potent pedagogical cocktail, one derived from Tony's own personal disposition as a teacher, as a special needs teacher, and as an ICT enthusiast within the notion of 'spaces for learning'. These are indicative of his learning trajectories as a mid-career teacher (Wenger, 1998); from a life history perspective, these are the distilled wisdom that he brings to bear on his teaching. As data analysis progressed, I began to construe this important complement of personal and professional characteristics as *crow's nest teaching*. Much of the remainder of this paper will be spent in illustrating how this is fashioned, and how it develops the agency of learners, with comment also on the structural location of this 'learning to labour' as well as learning to learn.

Crow's nest teaching

As many readers will know, the crow's nest is the lookout post atop the mast of a sailing ship, an important and crucial perch in the days before sonar radar etc. It enabled the 'look out' to see further on the horizon than colleagues 'below'. *crow's nest teaching* involves a panoramic view that encompasses learners and their needs, that embraces learning and the disposition of learners, in addition to a narrower focus on delivering a curriculum. Due to the particular circumstances of these learners, their own biographies, their previous experience of schooling, Tony was only too well aware of the incremental manner in which he had to build trust and relationships while gradually also giving more space to learners to exercise responsibility as they take responsibility for their own learning. An important point of entry in his pedagogical approach, that also displayed his vision, his perspective on his role as teacher, mentor, advocate, advisor and sometimes negotiator, was being an acute observer, where 'teachable moments' (Woods and Jeffrey 1996) were regularly exploited. An important feature of this was a blurring of boundaries, between informal and formal, between home and school, while also creating space for spontaneity and humour. The following extracts are illustrative.

Teachable moments: blurring boundaries between formal and informal

During the early morning when informal conversations pervade the classroom, while individuals bring their stories of happenings from the community and what is going on in their lives into the classroom conversation, Tony listens, often without comment, but seizes the moment to re-focus on more cognitive concerns. During the month of October, the boys were busy after school preparing for Halloween bonfires.

> At this point, Dan indicated that he (and his 'gang') had fifty pallets and three hundred tyres for the Halloween bonfire. Tony seized on the figures to ask Duncan if he gave one of the pallets to him, how many would be left. Even with the use of the hundred square, it was obvious that Duncan's grasp of number did not even come close to deducting one from fifty and getting forty-nine! Meantime, Margaret went to Jim's rescue at the bottom of the room, where he was drying his hands in his jacket after a trip to the toilet because the classroom towel had disappeared. With the informalities of the morning over, it was time to get down to mathematics—cards and worksheets.   (Field Notes)

Between Tony and Margaret, the SNA, there is evidence of a blend of care and cognition, of empathy with learners with an eye on the main chance, exploiting the borders between the formal and informal. Further blurring of boundaries between home and school creates spaces for humour and spontaneity, although managing such blurred boundaries was easier due to small numbers in the classroom. Nevertheless, boundaries premised on unusual levels of trust and positive relationships are cultivated, nurtured and constantly re-negotiated over time. The following extract is illustrative.

> Ben, who moments earlier had been 'cautioned' for interrupting other's stories, now commented on the bird's nest on a tree visible from the classroom window. There was an interesting set of exchanges. After someone mentioned a Magpie, Kenny piped up '... one for sorrow, two for joy' to which Kevin quickly replied, 'I don't believe that,' to nobody in particular. As ever, Tony tried to turn this gossip to a more structured conversation and inquired as to when birds build their nests. He received answers including Spring and Autumn, and when Kevin offered the correct response his neighbour, Dan quickly said, 'Put it there ... well done ...' and put his hand out to receive a high five but as Kevin was evidently about to reciprocate he quickly withdrew his hand saying, in that streetwise ironic tone, 'Get out of it'. (There is a level of street smarts and aggression about Dan's behaviour on occasion that does not make him a very likeable kid, but he's still a kid and he is emulating what he sees and hears from his 'bouncer' dad).   (Field Notes)

This final comment becomes significant later, when the transformative power of creative spaces for learning are the focus of attention. Teachable Moments (Woods and Jeffrey 1996) also exploited emergent and manufactured opportunities to provide positive reinforcement and feedback to the vulnerable learners whose self-image as learners were dented in their efforts to learn. Consequently, the affirmation of teachable moments was a very definite element of Tony's *crow's nest* view of where his pedagogy was leading incrementally. The following extract is illustrative.

> Meantime, Tony was showing short video clips on the Mac to which he'd added sound effects. Ben was delighted to see himself on the school stage displaying the skill of solo in hurling—over and back across the

stage, complete with cheers and applause! He was seriously proud of this 'excerpt'. Tony also indicated that here too was another possibility for lines of development for the class as they become more skilled in the use of ICT. He was, in a sense, pointing another way forward for those who were interested. Slowly, informally, but very deliberately, the curriculum is being 'rolled out' to maintain their interest as well as indicate possibilities.   (Field Notes)

Blurring boundaries

Meantime, as the following extracts illustrate, the spaces for learning created by Tony, enabled or facilitated the 'gang' in creating some continuity between 'street' and school, by providing more latitude for humour and language that would be much less likely to be tolerated in a mainstream classroom. It lent a positive quality to the learning environment that enabled them to feel more at home, while simultaneously creating potential negative consequences as they moved to their respective classrooms on a daily basis. As Arnot (2004) comments regarding Willis's classic study (*Learning to Labour*, 1977), there is an 'extraordinary conjunction of structural and subjective possibilities' that are brought together in this context, that are predominantly enabling in 'the unit' but are a source of conflict and marginalisation within the mainstream. Thus, within the one school, this blurring of boundaries has both positive and negative features. The following extract illustrates the spontaneity of learners, their humour that enables them to feel at home, while also making them resistant to the structural and pedagogical constraints imposed in mainstream classrooms. Kevin was not feeling well when he came to school, and he had been having difficulty with containing his pit bull dogs in his back garden as they had dug their way into the neighbours patch underneath the fence.

> Meanwhile, back in the classroom, Kevin was improving a little and I took the opportunity to inquire about the dogs. The fence has been erected in the back garden, but the 'dogs bit a fella' in part because 'he was kicking them'. Jim eaves dropping on this conversation remarks, 'Bit his arse ... oh me arse,' to which someone else chimed in, 'Bit his mickey'. Kevin, brightening up a little, asked, 'Who said this' and now that he had an audience, his sense of humour was being restored. He commented about getting up this morning and when I retorted jovially that he was

allergic to the morning, he replied with a smile, 'No allergic to school'.
... At this point Jim and himself got into some macho shadow boxing,
and as Kevin closed his fist and swung a 'haymaker' in Jim's general
direction, he remarked, 'You didn't see that did ya' in a friendly manner'.
(Field Notes)

Similarly, in the following exchange between Kenny and Dan, while the latter
provided assistance that is typical of many classroom encounters where peer
assistance, it is provided without fuss in a spontaneous manner and as this extract
reveals the kind of humorous exchange is more redolent of male workplace
humour than what one readily associates with primary classrooms!

While looking at some software, Kenny decided he wanted to print a
colour picture of a horse, and others repeated this. This suggests some
initiative on Kenny's part, while Dan had to be 'called in' to assist with
the printing. At one point, when the printer stubbornly refused to do his
bidding while making some labouring noises, he suggested, 'The printer's
playing with itself' ... further evidence of 'street talk' being imported in
a 'useful' manner into the classroom, but in a way that enhances rather
than disrupts learning.   (Field Notes)

In an initial mapping of the terrain of creative teaching and learning in this
context, there are two additional organising 'themes' beyond the *crow's nest*
disposition of the teacher that emerge as highly significant. Before moving
towards some tentative conclusions these will be briefly described and illustrated
with appropriate field note extracts, This approach I describe as a clustering or
confluence of various pedagogical strands that, when combined over time, lead
to 'moving up a gear': accelerated learning, and what I call the *Domestos factor*.
Transformative learning touches the self and identity of learners in ways that
more conventional pedagogies, or spaces for teaching rather than spaces for
learning, rarely if ever actually reach. Each will be described and illustrated in
turn, while it should be recognised also that in the present context, space does
not permit a more detailed and forensic analysis of all the nuances, subtleties
and detail.

'Moving up a gear': accelerated learning

We provide a brief elaboration of this concept before resorting to some field note extracts to illustrate it. It needs understanding against a backdrop of careful orchestration, on the teacher's part, from the beginning of the school year, to cultivate a positive and flexible learning atmosphere, underpinned by ongoing work on trust and relationships, while mindful of giving learners more latitude and responsibility to take more initiatives and risks in their own learning. The fruits of almost three months work, orchestrated from the teacher's view from the *crow's nest*, were now beginning to have its cumulative effect. The following field note extract seeks to capture a sense of this, when it says:

> One of the phrases that I'd recorded in earlier field notes was one used by Tony repeatedly—'moving up a gear'—to describe a kind of breakthrough on the part of an individual learner who was now reaching a kind of 'cruising' speed in terms of accelerated learning. This is all relative of course but the atmosphere in the classroom today was one of confidence, individual work in progress and a willingness on the part of the boys, all perhaps except Duncan, to 'show off' their work and accomplishments since our last encounter. Different individuals or pairs were repeatedly calling on me, more than in the past, to look at completed work, or work in progress. The general 'theme' for this set of notes, therefore, is 'moving up a gear'. (Field Notes)

In the same set of notes, the following more interpretive comments are provided that seek to indicate the cumulative impact of sustained commitment towards a particular view of teaching and learning, that, from the learners' perspectives, was evidently having the desired effect, whereby they were increasingly applying themselves in ways that made them authentic authors of their own learning.

> This may be construed as a particularly male metaphor, derived from an apparent male fascination with cars and speed, or from *Lego* and the importance of 'gearing up' moving parts to animate a construction and bring it to life. However, the general import seems to be a more Vygotskian notion of more independent learning—of being able to accomplish more on one's own as a consequence of scaffolded

support; that investments made earlier in the term in terms of personal relationships and incremental cognitive challenges were now beginning to have a cumulative effect. Evidence too perhaps that real learning takes time and with a group like this in particular, where unlearning previous negative encounters with learning and negative feedback with consequences for identity and self-esteem, takes more time to undo. Before such undoing can be turned to positive effect, where, it may be suggested, the previous foundations of learning must be undone and reformed so that learners have to 'turn a corner' before they are 'ready' to move up a gear.   (Field Notes)

Some weeks prior to this site visit, I had accompanied both special classes on a school outing that took in a visit to the Botanic Gardens, *McDonalds*, and a more opportunist visit to a playground. The latter became the subsequent focus of much work using *Lego*, to construct motorised features of a playground that entailed sophisticated programming for animation. What is very evident in the following extract is that there was a new found confidence in the learners that was also apparent in their body language, their work ethic, and other important aspects of their own learning that I tried to capture in the notes.

Three of the boys in particular, Dan, Kevin and Ben, definitely presented as having 'moved up a gear', their whole body language is remarkably different, especially the first two. Dan, has an air of confidence and importance, smiles more and is more friendly towards the others, where previously he was inclined to scowl, and adopt a more hostile 'posture' towards the others—this is something of a transformation. Kevin has sort of blossomed—he has much more 'pep in his step' and an openness in his face, and a willingness to contribute and participate that is in sharp contrast to earlier 'refusals' and reluctance to step outside his protective cocoon. His artistic skills are in much demand at present. He spent some of the morning in the other learning support room painting the canvas backdrop for the Christmas concert. His handy work is evident also in the school foyer. On one side is a substantial crib while a streetscape has been constructed on the other and Kevin has contributed in this context. Meanwhile, back in his classroom, he has used the photographs that Dan took of trees reflected in water in the Botanic Gardens as the basis of very credible still life pictures/ paintings. However, he has 'moved on' also in his use of *Lego* and spent some time showing me how he programmed an RCX to 'drive' his playground. Time spent in the playground has been the catalyst for a plethora of fun parks that others too were busy constructing and adding refinements.   (Field Notes)

There was a genuine enthusiasm for this kind of work facilitated by the teacher but directed and led by the learners and fuelled by observations of one another's work. However, there was also an infectious character to the various efforts, while the space also allowed for the setting of an individual pace of work. The following extract provides additional evidence that creative learning is cumulative but not quite linear because acceleration of pace is injected into the process at certain points propelling the learner into a different orbit. Several aspects of the teaching process converge and have impact all at once; a happy confluence that enables the learner to 'move up a gear' in his own learning. Dan, as indicated earlier was a reluctant learner with a tendency to be a bully, but was transformed suddenly into a different kind of learner.

Dan demonstrates most dramatically that he has 'moved up a gear'. First, on our outing he took to his photography assignment like the proverbial duck to water. He began the day by showing me the photographs that he'd taken, now all carefully stored in his folder on the PC, and he was very comfortable navigating back and forth while talking about the photographs etc. There was a new contentment in his voice as well as satisfaction at his accomplishment. However, he had also built a playground with four 'geared' items all of which he had powered by an RCX that he'd programmed. Tony spent some time with him, helping him to refine the programming, and at one time Ben was called on to show him how he could remove or add an item, something that he demonstrated on screen with aplomb. Tony immediately complimented Ben for remembering what was involved, while Dan 'copied' the moves with accomplished ease. The exchange of skills and expertise was casual and matter of fact, no fuss and each went back to their own tasks instantly as if the encounter had never occurred—such was the, taken for granted, aspect of this peer/peer support, under the watchful eye of the 'master'. Dan spent the entire morning, almost ninety minutes 'playing' with his work during which time he dealt with issue of rotation, music and reversing sea saws etc., sophisticated work in which he was engrossed and

> his new found contentment and status was palpable—a 'happy camper'
> in ways that were not previously evident.   (Field Notes)

The extract also seeks to capture other significant elements of creative learning
that are particularly significant for this group of learners. There is evidence of
prolonged engagement, tenacity and a willingness to tinker with things in pursuit
of their own learning quite independently of the teacher. They also recognise that
help is at hand from the teacher, or a peer, should the need arise, something that
encourages and fosters a degree of risk-taking that would be unlikely to occur
in other circumstances. However, while this level of support does not intrude
into their own particular learning space that is sheltered within a larger harbour
of teaching and learning.

These characteristics of creative learning manifest here, are in part basis for
as well as contributing to what I have labelled the 'Domestos factor.

The Domestos factor: transforming learner's self and identity

I am confident that this aspect of creative teaching and learning could be
illustrated by reference to any one of the learners in this classroom in somewhat
different ways, while the key characteristics of this transformative impact are
consistent. It is in this context also that a judicious mix of life history and
ethnography combines in particularly powerful ways to dig deeper into what
might be termed more surface manifestations. I have chosen Ben and his
biography to illustrate the impact on self-esteem of creative learning through
a combination of external affirmation and intrinsic rewards and the way it
transforms the learner. The impact of such spaces for learning is that the learner
begins to experiment with a new persona, while the learning opportunities and
the engagement this facilitates, creates space to experiment with wearing this
new self-image while seeking to shape a new identity.

Ben comes from a seriously dysfunctional family where violence and verbal
outrage are the means of settling disputes. He was in a mainstream classroom
last year and was perpetually in trouble as a disruptive force—loud, brash and
difficult. In a staffroom conversation one morning before formal school began,
he was described by his former class teacher as 'mad' and he went on to heap
opprobrium on him and his family, to which some other colleagues seemed
only too happy to contribute. He was summoned before the school's Board of
Management prior to being suspended and during the course of this 'interview'
he was threatened with the possibility of incarceration in an industrial school

if he did not mend his ways. Safe to say then that Ben was no stranger to controversy, and earlier in the year he had had infrequent skirmishes with the teacher in the mainstream class which he attends daily. He is bright and has a very strong sense of fairness.

There is a buddy system in operation between the boys in the 'senior' special class, and their junior colleagues, and Ben in particular takes his responsibility for Ross very seriously. Ross is the youngest of the boys in the junior class and during 'breakfast' each day, Ben sits and talks with him, and generally takes a very active interest in his welfare. Margaret has spoken repeatedly of this gentler side to Ben's persona that is often not very apparent. In turn, when he has been in 'trouble' with his mainstream teacher, Tony has invested considerable time and energy counselling him, always with an eye to getting him to control his temper, to walk away rather than 'lose it' as he frequently puts it. Ben's engagement, work ethic, responsibility, persistence are all evident in the next extract, the cumulative impact of carefully orchestrated teaching and learning from the *crow's nest* since the beginning of this voyage with Tony as skipper. Now, Ben is an experienced deck hand who willingly goes to work in pursuit of his own learning. It is as if the advocacy that Tony extends to Ben, when needed, mirrors Ben's emerging relationship with Ross.

> Ben sat with Ross, played with him and generally looked out for him. Some time later when we were back in the classroom and viewing the video that Tony had recorded of our 'outing.' In an early part of the clip, where Sarah, our guide (in the Botanic Gardens) asked about the classes represented. Ben piped up and added 'junior infants' for, after all, his buddy Ross was the only junior infant there, but his care and concern extended to making sure that Ross's presence was 'noted' by the guide.
> (Field Notes)

On our return to the 'senior' classroom, and the learners went about their respective learning, the notes capture Ben as follows:

> Nearby, Ben was 'tinkering' with his fun park and quietly singing to himself. He was singing *in excelsis deo*. Having listened for a while so as not to intrude, I commented, only to learn that this was no idle warbling as he informed me that he was 'rehearsing' for the school choir which is performing in the concert. Ben is rapidly accumulating 'successes' on a

number of fronts that, for the moment at least, are transforming him into an individual with a very positive learning trajectory. However, this fragile house of cards could tumble down.   (Field Notes)

Ben has found a different voice through his learning, whereas his voice until recently had been shrill and loud in attempt to gain attention and recognition. He is trying on a new identity for size, while the world beyond the creative learning space co-constructed by his peers, with Tony as skipper and Margaret as first mate, frequently constrain and impede this learning trajectory. The previous habits of learning ensure that the mask slips and elements of the earlier identity become more pronounced. However, from the point of view of this particular theme, what is evident is that these spaces, and the learning opportunities they create, reach into the psyche, self and identity of learners in ways that more conventional teaching doesn't attempt nor does it reach the self of the learner.

The primary focus of this paper has been on the agency of teacher and learners, while there has been occasional reference to structural location and the constraints and complications created by a creative pedagogy located on the margins. In particular, learners occupy and actively participate in creating and shaping this space, and engage in daily border crossings between this 'space' and the space that is their mainstream classrooms. Not surprisingly, on several occasions, they found excuses to return rapidly from the mainstream, and on others, pleaded to remain and found excuses to be allowed to do so, on the pretext of having work to complete. It was obvious from many such exchanges that they clearly sought to exercise a preference for the environment created by Sir Tony. Their own estimation was that the 'unit' was much more conducive to creative learning but it also highlighted for them and brought into high relief, the typical constraints frequently imposed by the mainstream. Thus, their creative encounters tended to marginalise them while being a positive learning experience. Suffice to say that the three learners who graduated from Strumpet City school in June 2004 were about to enter the local secondary school in September where there is no special class provision. This realisation is a stark reminder of the marginal space that such learners occupy within the system of schooling, although there is much more that could be told about this aspect of their schooling experience.

Conclusions

There is much more detail in the data than it is possible to deal with in one paper. In a general manner, this paper has attempted to capture three major themes of creative teaching and learning as manifest in this teacher's work. Significantly, the first *crow's nest teaching* deals primarily with the disposition of the teacher and the kind of pedagogical strategies deployed to create a particularly conducive learning environment that is shaped significantly by context, as well as the biographies of teacher and learners. The other two themes—while not ignoring the stance of the teacher, his positioning on the bridge of the enterprise, and the navigational strategies he deploys to provide a rudder for learning and the spaces for learning he creates—are conducive to learners' exercising their agency as well as charting their own learning interests and trajectories. Yet, one is left with a sense that this is possible precisely because both the teacher and the learners are positioned on the periphery of the schooling system. Thus, from this marginal position it is possible to evade and ignore the more prescriptive curriculum content and attendant pedagogies of the mainstream. While many of the characteristics of creative teaching and learning illustrated and illuminated here resonate with the work of others, it is important to note also the agency of learners themselves in the process. Further analysis of this aspect of the work awaits attention, but it has potential to be an important addition to work on creative teaching and learning. The initial analysis presented here is but a start, but sufficiently encouraging to warrant considerable further attention, as well as the tensions between structure and agency. Even if creative teaching and learning occupy marginal spaces within the education system, it nevertheless has potential to educate, and even in a somewhat subversive manner, undermine more orthodox teaching and learning. I share with Willis his sense of the 'importance of getting a store of data that you could go through later' (Mills and Gibb, 2004). The mining of this rich vein of material continues.

References

Arnot, M. (2004) Male working class identities and social justice, in Dolby, N., Dimitriadis, G. and Willis, P. (ed.) *Learning to Labour in New Times*, New York and London: Routledge Falmer.

Carey, P. (2000) *True History of the Kelly Gang*, London: Faber and Faber.

Corcoran, M. P. and Peillon, M. (eds) (2002) *Ireland Unbound, A Turn of the Century Chronicle*, Dublin: Institute of Public Administration.

Fitzgerald, G. (1991) *All in a Life. Garrett Fitzgerald, An Autobiography*, Dublin: Gill and Macmillan.

Fullan, M. (2003) *Change Forces with a Vengeance*, New York and London: Routledge Falmer.

Giddens, A. (1991) *Modernity and Self-Identity, Self and Society in the Late Modern Age*, Stanford: Stanford University Press.

Goodson, I. F. and Sikes, P. (eds) (2001) *Life History Research In Educational Settings*, Buckingham and Philadelphia: Open University Press.

Government of Ireland, (1999) *Primary School Curriculum Introduction*, Dublin: Government Publications.

Hargreaves, A. (2003) *Teaching in the Knowledge Society*, Buckingham: Open University Press.

Homer-Dixon, T. (2001) *The Ingenuity Gap*, Toronto: Vintage Canada.

Labaree, D. F. (2004) *The Trouble with Ed Schools*, New Haven and London: Yale University Press.

Lee, J. J. (1989) *Ireland 1912-1985 Policies and Society*, Cambridge: Cambridge University Press.

Lynch, K. and Lodge, A. (2002) *Equality and Power in Schools*, London and New York: Routledge/Falmer.

Mills D. and Gibb, R. (2004), Centre and Periphery—An Interview with Pual Willis, in Dolby, N., Dimitriadis, G. and Willis, P. (eds) *Learning to Labour in New Times*, New York and London: Routledge Falmer.

O'Connell, M. (2001) *Changed Utterly. Ireland and the New Irish Psyche*, Dublin: The Liffey Press.

Oatley, K. and Jenkins, J. (1998) *Understanding Emotions*, Oxford: Blackwell Publishers Ltd.

OECD. (1991) *Reviews of National Education Policies for Education, Ireland*, Paris: OECD.

Sugrue, C. (1996) Student Teachers' Lay Theories, Implications for professional development, in Goodson, I. F. and Hargreaves, A. (eds) *Teachers' Professional Lives*, London: Falmer Press.

Sugrue, C. (1997) *Complexities of Teaching, Child-centred Perspectives*, London: Falmer Press.

Sugrue, C. (ed.) (2004). *Curriculum and Ideology, Irish Experiences, International Perspectives*, Dublin: The Liffey Press.

Thompson, P. (2002) *Schooling the Rustbelt Kids making the difference in changing times*, Stoke on Trent: Trentham Books.

Troman, G. and Woods, P. (2001) *Primary Teachers' Stress*, London and New York: Routledge Falmer.

Wenger, E. (1998) *Communities of Practice*, Cambridge: Cambridge University Press.

Willis, P. (1977) *Learning to Labour, How Working Class Kids Get Working Class Jobs*, Aldershot: Gower Publishing Company.

Woods, P. (1995) *Creative Teachers in primary schools*, Buckingham: Open University Press.

Woods, P. (1996) *Researching The Art of Teaching, Ethnography for educational use*, London and New York: Routledge.

Woods P. and Jeffrey B (1996) *Teachable Moments, Buckingham: The Open University Press*

New learning strategies in the upper secondary school: The Danish fieldwork in IT classes

Karen Borgnakke
University of Odense, Denmark

The main objectives are to identify teachers' and students' strategies for developing creative learning in educational contexts. In relation to these objectives the Danish fieldwork and case studies are focusing on 'new learning strategies and new teaching practices in the Gymnasium in terms of IT based learning and project work'.

The focus has been firstly on the question of how the school uses IT based learning, project work and problem based strategies to improve development, secondly on the question of what characterises the repertoire of action in these teaching and learning situations, and thirdly on an examination of the learners' views and perceptions of their learning experiences.

The fieldwork has been carried out by means of observations, conversations, interviews and material collected relating to three school levels:

1)   the leader level (interview with the head and the management team)
2)   the colleague/teacher level (interviews with the teacher group associated with the observed classes)
3)   the level of teaching and learning practices (observation and interview with groups of students)

Research strategies and models have been developed by Borgnakke (1996, 2000, 2004b) and are characterised as intensive field work based on the classic ethnographic framework and renewed models. The classic framework is described in Educational Field research (Borgnakke1996) where I present an overall, deep description of the fieldwork with detailed analyses of the practical context and the learning processes involved.[1]

With this background I concentrated the renewed fieldwork and its empirical potentials on social and cultural studies of learning. But even though classic fieldwork seems to be a good methodological answer it needs new categorical thinking about learning and educational cultures in late modernity. Against this background I show the potential for intensive and comparative fieldwork closely

---

1 The empirical and analytic conceptualising of learning derives from my main research project Studies in Learning—a late modern challenge. The theoretical investigations involved and the range of related research projects are described in Borgnakke 2003.

related to the CLASP projects and my fieldwork in IT classes (Borgnakke, 2004b).

The CLASP projects were planned as intensive fieldwork done in phases during September 2003 to June 2004. The phases with participant observation at the different school levels meant day-to-day observation and comparative studies in two classes. The observations cover routines in teaching and learning as well as activities chosen by the students and the teachers as examples of new learning strategies and new teaching practices.

These school studies at the upper secondary level are related to a broader educational and political context, both in terms of ethnographic research and in terms of evaluation and development work.

The political and practical context: Development of the upper secondary school

In a political sense the context is characterised by major national programmes for development. These programmes have an impact on those sectors related from early schooling in the middle of 1980s to adult education and to the Danish compulsory school. The actual national programme, dating from 1999, is aimed at youth education and the upper secondary school, the Danish Gymnasium. This programme demonstrates (Borgnakke, 2004a), firstly, education policy and the demands of new strategies for learning, teaching and evaluation. Secondly the programme demonstrates the need for the organisational development of new strategies for teacher teams and leadership. Thirdly the programme mirrors the development through the last decades and the changing discourse from elite to mass education. A sociological overview of the decades and change is given in former research projects on the Upper Secondary School by Adrian (1980) and Rasmussen (1998).[2]

These changes have had an impact on the social key questions of class, ethnicity and gender, both in terms of international education policy and in terms of national reforms and pedagogical consequences. We can recognise how the political agenda and ideas derive from the international policy level in the OECD and European Union. At a national level in the Nordic countries we can see almost the same political discourse and reform tendencies, though reforms at upper secondary level, both in Norway and Sweden, have already been implemented (Beach and Dovemark, 2004, Dovemark, 2004).

2 The description is given in Borgnakke (1996). The methodological issue is systematically reflected in Borgnakke (1996c)..

The Danish reform of The Gymnasium will be implemented in 2005. The Upper Secondary level of education typically begins at the end of full-time compulsory education. This level also divides into: 1. General education qualifying for access to higher education; and 2. Commercial or technical education, also a qualifier for access to the labour market. The CLASP projects fieldwork has been carried out in the general Gymnasium. Related case studies have been done in the commercial and technical Gymnasium. The main point is that the programme and the coming reform of upper secondary education represent the political context.[3]

In a pedagogical sense project pedagogy has been the main current that runs through reforms and alternative models for education and learning in the Danish context. The principles of project pedagogy are project organisation, interdisciplinary work, problem solving, participant management and exemplary learning. These principles have a broad theoretical background and have links to the ideas of Piaget (1969) and Vygotsky (1962/82)—not to mention, of course, Dewey (1902/90, 1910/91). This theoretical background has been a starting point for an ongoing process of rethinking and renewal. The renewals could have their basis in Negt's reformulation of exemplary learning and sociological imagination (Negt, 1971) and be linked to adult education, or they could be associated with youth education as inspired by Ziehe's diagnosis of new youth cultures (Ziehe, 1982, 1987). Further other aspects of project work and its principles are linked to new concepts of learning and creativity (Olsen, 1992, Langager, 1994, Kupferberg, 1996).[4] While renewal of these principles is sharpening the perspective of learning, the major issues concern the ways in which the principles are implemented and interpreted in practical use. Analysis by Borgnakke (1996, 1998, 2004c, 2005) of the related political discourse and practical interpretation shows periodic shifts in which one or other of the principles takes the leading role. Sometimes the principles of interdisciplinary work and the demands of cross-curricular activity predominate, while at others, the principles of problem orientation and problem solving prevail. It is often stressed that something is missing. The principles of participant management and exemplary learning, in particular, are at risk of being the missing link in practical and organisational interpretation.

3 One of the CLASP projects has been related to critical and empirical studies on the education policy and new school practice in Sweden, see Beach (2004), Beach and Dovemark (2004) and Dovemark (2004)
4 With references to the political texts, development works and evaluative reports the impact of the programme is described in Beck et al. 2003..

At university level the modern reform universities, first Roskilde University Center, then Aalborg University, are the institutions where project pedagogy has been both official and most effectively realised. In general Danish educational reform programmes have a tradition of experimental and developmental work expressed by the principles of project pedagogy and by different forms of renewal of the basic principle, *learning by doing.*

In the present educational context project, work involves both a work process and a learning process, described as creative learning and IT learning strategies at the upper secondary level. My fieldwork in the general Gymnasium concentrated on IT based learning and can be conceptualised both in terms of the progressive tradition and experiences from the seventeenth century (Adrian et al., 1980) and in terms of the newest experiences from The Virtual School. The related case studies on project work taking place in the commercial and technical Gymnasium are a part of a tradition for what Borgnakke (2004c, 2005) describes as the practice and profession oriented project work.[5]

The tendencies mentioned and their impact on the Upper Secondary School are the context for this fieldwork and at the same time refer to the practical school level and to the national programmes of development, in which one of the aims is to enhance:

> ... more students activating teaching and working forms with implementation of information technology and new forms of evaluation, and in all senses new forms of organisation of the students work to improve both personal qualification and subject competencies.
>
> (Ministry of Education, 1999)

In a practical sense schools show how national programmes and reforms are implemented. But each school has the autonomy to select its own particular profile and development work, just as groups of teachers have the autonomy to select particular themes or combinations of subjects over the year. In the light of this autonomy the school's involvement in *The Electronic School* and IT based learning programmes has to be seen as their strategic choice for school development.

---

5   The first introductions were focused on the principles and organisational matters, see Illeris (1981). Later discussions incorporate creativity, see Olsen (1993) and Kupferberg (1996) and linked to educational experiments Langager (1994).

The Electronic School—the learning context for IT classes

The school has about four hundred and fifty students and fifty-six teachers and is placed in a suburb south of Copenhagen. The school has a multi-ethnic profile, forty per cent of the students have a cultural background which is not Danish. Besides being involved with development of *The Electronic School*, the school has also recently started a programme in multimedia and film studies.

The classes observed—and in focus—are the so-called IT classes, where the observations are concentrated on two classes: 1.G (ages sixteen to seventeen) and 3.G (ages eighteen to nineteen). During the period when I carried out observations, September to December, 2003, I had access to all kinds of school activities among the two groups of teachers and students. The observations, material collected and interviews were organised in phases shifting between school levels and between the two classes. The empirical data and materials cover, therefore, the school at the three levels as well as the process of teaching and learning in the IT classes.[6] The observations and interviews show here how the students in 1.G class create strategies for IT learning as *newcomers*, while learning strategies in the 3.G class are rather re-created by the students as *old-timers*.[7]

At an organisational level *The Electronic School* is already a part of the current programme of reform as well as being an experienced part of the pedagogical development of creative teaching and learning. It is a central point that my fieldwork identifies the pedagogical tendencies and practical results at all three levels, though the leader level is the starting point for capturing the school as a whole.

A school in transition –the story of management and staff

The management level as covered by written materials and interviews speaks of the school's history and its special profile and development work. The material shows how the school has changed its strategy. As the head of the school says,

> We no longer take part in those huge and fancy experiments. It is more important for us that we are involved in 'the new tendencies' like IT learning on an everyday basis and in ordinary conditions.

---

6   The important tendencies from 1970-2000 are further described at different levels from the Danish Folkeskole to the university level in Borgnakke (1995, 1998a).
7   The distinction between *newcomers* and *old-timers* is inspired by Lave and Wenger (1991). The empirical background for the study of learning strategies is my own fieldwork and the detailed analysis of learning processes given in Borgnakke (1996).

The material also shows how the strategy influences the process of reprofessionalising the teaching staff. The strategy involves some of the teachers getting formal education, for example a master's degree in IT Education. However, the main point is that the whole staff receives training as non-formal 'in service training'. The pedagogical challenge is, according to the head, that all school levels are to be looked upon as being 'in practical transition' not occupied with 'fancy experiments' but rather by 'everyday school life and experience'.

As regards the background, the head talks about the local conditions being distanced from with the educational tradition connected to the traditional Gymnasium. The head talks about the schools start in the seventies:

> There were only three cultural institutions in this area: The Church, The Gymnasium and The Library. In a sense that is somehow a starting point for building up a school. Then there is a long period of time, where you not only recognised all the new people coming into the school, you also needed to work with the people. This shows that we, maybe innocently, started to create a new pedagogy to hold those people. I mean it is not these kinds of people you can read about in the textbooks. I think this pedagogical development is similar to one described in Italy as 'the integrating background'. You use the people living here and you need to use their background to establish education and teaching. You use their qualifications, their way of thinking, life forms and cultural background.

The school believes that it needs to consider the resources relating to 'The White' and 'The Black' students in order to make them available to the students and their different cultural backgrounds. As the head says, there is always a risk that, 'the White will escape, when impacts from the Black become more obvious.' And therefore, as the head continues;

> We offer activities and make sure that 'The White' pupils do not escape.'

The offer of IT classes, where every student gets his own laptop has to be seen in this light as have the processes of implementation of IT based strategies and enhancing teachers' qualifications. As the head says:

The question I have been asked the most from my principal colleagues is 'How do you do it, because we cannot get our teachers on board?' I say, I don't know, but they probably got an offer they couldn't refuse! And I must say that it strikes all my colleagues as surprising that it is possible to fire up such an old teaching staff. It was not even difficult, maybe because we decided not to accept the stereotype of 'Black Trash' being applied to students—we simply would not accept that—and that is why we were forced to do something.

In this sense the school and the teaching staff was 'forced' to be a learning organisation with a practical policy for in service training courses in IT. As the head says:

> Our policy was that everyone in the staff should learn IT for use in their teaching. We did not want an 'A and B team'—therefore all the teachers have been through courses in IT. We are proud that we don't have a B-team—or at least that it's a small one.

Another member of the management group adds:

> We have educated one another. Those who started in 1997 did so with a training course as distance learning. They became super users and afterwards created courses for the rest of the teachers.

According to the head the strategy was not an experiment with 'fancy words and goal setting' and as he says:

> To be safe in the school means that 'no one runs away screaming' when we throw The Lap Top Project into the air. At the same time it was accepted that in service training not dealing with IT was closed down. You could not go to a course in 'French verbs'.

This staff strategy created the feeling among the teachers of being safe. For the school it was both a mark of identity and a challenge to cope with the electronic environment.

The key question for the challenge was, how could laptops be used in the process of teaching and learning, to make practical sense? At this point the process of implementation was teacher-directed. To grasp the results, empirical materials from the practical school levels must be taken in account. Interviews with teachers and analysis on the staff level show how they talk about their own way of learning to manage IT tools and projects. Observations of teachers' instruction and interactions with the students show how they create the new IT management and its products as a part of the new routine for teaching in a classroom. But the observations also show how more public activities are created in the light of a new school and in the context of youth culture. Literally speaking classes and students perform not in a classroom but on a stage and show results from work with this new technology and with film production.

Teaching strategies

The observation has identified teacher strategies for developing creative learning in classroom activities as well as activities in the group and project work. The new strategies I will describe as variations of ideal types: the classic lecture, traditional classroom teaching, group work and project work. In upper secondary institutions there is mainly traditional classroom teaching. This applies also in the observed IT classes. Against this background my analysis shows how the lap-top is integrated in traditional teaching strategies. A simple example could be History or Danish lessons where the textbook is downloaded and therefore exists as a teaching text on the computer. In these situations the teaching strategy is traditional but at the same time optimised by the variety of textbook materials. At the other end of the spectrum, against the background of group work and project work, my analyses show how teacher and students are experimenting with the new possibilities. One example is the Middle Ages Project—a virtual inter-Nordic IT project (on medieval work, culture, religion etc.) The 1.G students worked in groups together with teachers and students from Iceland and Norway. The project work results observed are new genres covered as a *PowerPoint* collection and a *Net Newspaper*'(*Svaneavisen*). My analysis of this course is concentrated on the challenges relating to: 1. team teaching on the internet—organisational challenges and difficulties; 2. taking ownership and group leadership—among the students/among the learners; and 3. a *PowerPoint* collection—new aesthetics norms and standards for learning products.

The Danish teachers' own evaluations confirm these challenges. The teachers even talked about them as 'the new demands' and 'the new teacher skills' related to optimising the teachers' collaborative skills and experiences. The teachers underlined the technical and practical issues connected to the project and its character of virtuality. But against the same virtual background it also became clearer that physical presence was needed. As one of the teachers stressed:

> It is an absolute necessity that *each and every one* in the group of participating teachers meet physically and plan the project in details.

Related to developing the role as supervisor close to the process, I noted the same need to underline the teacher's presence. The teacher evaluation even mentioned the general need for a support teacher.

> The optimal form would be a support teacher in the intensive writing/ supervising course. One of the ideas behind the written work in Danish is precisely that the students should learn by being corrected and supervised during the process instead of after it.

During the project this shows up as the primary requirement for a good communicator to be available. According to the teachers, the students succeeded, as was stated in the evaluation:

> Difficulties we have overcome: The language barrier—three different languages. It has been positive to see the students *communicate*—not necessarily correctly in linguistic terms, but nevertheless very effectively.

The virtual project was extremely advanced by being a new kind of IT based project work. On one hand the project demands creativity and experience and makes demands which exceed what the group of teachers and 1.g students were able to give at the time. On the other hand this shortfall provides the challenge.

The next example, on the contrary, is the result of implementation and adaptation to better known teaching strategies.

The observation of teaching and learning among the students in the 3.g IT classes has to be regarded as observation of *old-timers*. The students know the routine in the IT class from the inside. A reconstruction based on day-to-day observation and interviews with teacher and students shows the new routines in a very concrete manner. There are several important empirical findings but primarily the reconstruction concentrated on the spirit of the experienced group of students: 'We are beyond…' (as the 3.g class and groups of students told me) 'the phase of impression and using the computer all the time'. The 3.G students are also 'beyond the childish surfing on the internet, private chat and hidden play sessions during the lesson'.

The students are doing 'IT based learning' and using the computer in a mix with other classroom activities, oral presentations and discussions, where the interesting part, in an empirical sense too, is 'the mix'. This mix, literally speaking, means that the whole spectrum of ideal types is used though in short versions. There is, for example, the classic lecture, as short as fifteen minutes, in which the teacher in Danish gives a sketch of Romanticism as an idea and cultural history, then moves to the main text of the day, tales from the great story-teller, Hans Christian Andersen. The students have the Andersen texts and their own work on the computer, and their homework pops up on the screens. In this situation we see the teacher in action as classroom teacher and lap-top coordinator. Twenty minutes later there is some mini group work, with students showing *PowerPoint* and *Actant* models on the screen.

Creative learning—characteristics

As described in Borgnakke (1996, 2000, 2004b), my former fieldwork covers the whole spectrum of teaching and learning strategies, including analysis of learning processes and students' own strategies. My analysis shows how the cardinal point in the process represents not only challenges but also basic difficulties related to the learning strategies involved in project work (Borgnakke, 1998). According to the learners this concerns a dilemma between the reproductive and the independent productive and creative aspects of their learning process. Furthermore it relates to conflicts between building up subject and topic-oriented basic knowledge and the development of the project oriented reflection and problem consciousness. This distinction, between learners' reproduction and production on the one hand and between learners' building up basic knowledge/ problem consciousness on the other, refers to the very basis of conceptualising learning. Therefore the current fieldwork, covering the different learning situations and phases, also provides examples of phases of reproduction and phases of creative production. The examples range from simple reproduction to sophisticated creation, and we can take these quite literally. Take, for instance, the situation where two students are working on their Middle Ages Project, both sitting with the computer in front of them. One says, 'We need a little bit more about power, the church and maybe the buildings ...' The other student is already on the net accessing a text-document in their common sources, copying and pasting a part of a text, saying, 'Yeah, we have it here. Look! Are you satisfied?'

This short course in learning was a course in reproduction pure and simple. What I saw popping up on the screen was 'a copy' and the students did not quote, they reproduced the text book as their own text. But at the same time it was characteristic for this group as well as for the other one I observed that there were also phases of very sophisticated creativity. Though connected to creating a *PowerPoint* collection, it was a matter of building up new basic knowledge (facts and knowledge about the Middle Ages) and problem consciousness, developing meta-reflections about the common theme and the project as a whole and about communication on the net with the other Nordic members. That means that even though the basic dilemma between reproduction and creative production still has impact, we also need to see the dilemma as a dynamic and driving force. Furthermore my field notes recall other basic conflicts and dynamic contrasts like desire/duty, play/learning, leisure ('for leisure use')/school ('for school use'). The interesting part is not the conflict or the concept in it self but rather the practical consequences. Teacher and students refer to the contrast and put it into words. The contrast lies furthermore in the fundamental grounding of IT classes, in the architecture, and seems to be the driving force for the process of learning. The contrasts (and even the students' choice of words and metaphors) appear again in their own statements, if the students get closer to the important issues. This is the case, for example, when one of the students in a long conversation with me about his use of the personal computer, summarises his statement as:

> It is about the feeling, where you want to go to school. I enjoy going to school more when we, as in the IT classes, have our own computers. It is more fun, pure and simple.

In an analytic sense this kind of statement is one of the big and basic ones. If students in the Gymnasium, like the rest of youth in late modernity, have been in school settings their whole lives, and then all of a sudden enjoy their school time more, one must acknowledge that, seen from a student perspective, the use of computers in schools is much more than a matter of text, screen and a printer. But if a student uses the words 'desire', 'want to', 'enjoy' or 'fun', s/he does not delete the co-existence of duty and the perspective of duty. Basically the point, therefore, is strictly related to the conflict and the dynamic between desire/duty, play/learning, leisure (and 'for leisure use')/school (and 'for school use').

The progression in observation demands concrete examples of creativity in learning processes. The best examples are related to the experienced IT students from 3.G and their way of doing computer based homework, assignments or receiving feedback from the teacher; or examples coming from the virtual project on the Middle Ages. According to the students these would represent creativity in learning both as a visible product and an ongoing process.

The process of learning and questions about how the students' reflect upon their learning are a vital part of the observations and ongoing talks with students. But one 'case' and material collected from observations in 3.G. classes are of special interest and exemplary character, namely a collection of essays on the theme of learning. All the students have given in a four to five page 'essay' as an answer to the question, 'How I learn—experiences from my IT class'. There is also another collection (though smaller) from 1.G. students where they evaluate (in a two page scheme) their experiences with project work and problem based learning, based on The Middle Ages Project. These, together with interviews and conversations with students on the common theme of new learning strategies, confirm the main impression of better conditions for creative learning in IT classes. There would also be examples from formal and scheduled creative learning.

Nevertheless, I would like to give an example of non-formal learning and unexpected creativity, namely learning through a strike. At the same time my point is to exemplify how creativity is a vital aspect of any learning processes. Whether creativity is on the official agenda or not, learning new 'stuff', new skills etc. implies 'being creative', if we look at the process from the learner's perspective. In this sense the learner's creativity shows up in its impact on all the empirical materials coming from the students, though some examples show it in an exemplary manner. In my case even the first day of observation shows it as a surprise. The observation was concerned with the daily routine and every day life in school. But when I showed up the situation was quite the opposite. It was not an ordinary day or even a school day. The students were on strike. They had occupied the school and closed the door in a very real and symbolic manner as I describe it in the field note below.

> I arrive at the school in good time (a fieldworker must not be late!) and I wonder why I can see so many students arriving all too early. There are chairs blocking the main door, and on a sign is written, 'Teachers no admittance'.
>
> 'Are you a teacher?' the young people behind the window ask me.

'No,'I say,'I have a project on the school, where I will be in the classes for the next couple of months, making observations and interviews.'

'You can't go in. We are on strike,'they tell me.

Me:'I'm here to get the project started and to follow one of the 1.G. classes. I don't think I can just leave without having talked to students about why you are on strike. Can I talk to your spokesman?'

A new person (this time a girl) comes to the door. We start a conversation about the strike, but neither of us can really hear what the other is saying. The students say, laughing: 'We will let you in. This is too stupid.'

And then I was inside, and the only adult in the building—apart from the caretaker and AB (the principal), who also happen to be on site.

The students give me a briefing on the programme of the day. The students are to:

1) get together in the canteen, listen to speeches from 'one from DGS' (Danish Association of Upper Secondary Students), make banners;

2) walk all together to N. Gymnasium, escorted by the police; and

3) walk again to the county house.

As the students tell me: 'It is all against the cuts. We are striking for the teachers and the school, too, not only for our own benefit.' They suggest that I wait in the canteen, hanging out to see what will happen.

Suddenly we can hear one shout, 'AB is in the building.' 'A mistake,' mumble others. 'One of the blunders,' another comments. The students start running towards one of the other entrances, which needs to be blocked better. I get into the canteen where groups of students have just arrived. The time is almost 8 a. m. Students are coming, picking a chair and sitting on the first level close to the stage.

Apropos 'AB'. One asks: 'Is AB still in the building?'

Another answers, 'Yes, but it is OK. He is with us.'   (Field Notes)

As the field notes illustrate we are dealing with examples and situations where the students in all senses take ownership, control, create and make their own decisions. Furthermore the students in both a concrete and symbolic manner are gatekeepers. To enter, one must have the students' permission and from the start the students denied anybody looking like an adult teacher access to the school. 'Teachers no admittance', the sign on the door said. At the same time the indoor localities became crowded with people and a number of activities are going to start. There is a plenary discussion and group work, different organisational possibilities and activities have to be planned, directed and carried out. There are no doubts that it is a day without teachers or teacher direction. The whole point is that the students all by themselves organise and lead the battle. While doing it, they bring teacher/student roles and relations to mind. And on a day like this, the students are not referring to themselves as 'students' or 'pupils', but as people, individuals or human beings! As the leader of the strike said from the stage when he summed up the day: 'Five hundred people were gathered at N. Gymnasium ...'

The day is without teachers, students and obviously without teaching. But the day is not without learning. Whether we want to call it learning-from-a-strike or learning in democracy or just 'non-formal learning' is not important. But it is certainly *learning by doing*. My field notes from the following days also provide many references to life skills and student development. I write, for instance, about and use words such as 'organisational skills' or the young students' 'media skills'. Likewise the field notes expressed situations with the active group of 1.G students in terms like, 'They are growing before my eyes.'

To come that close to the situation and 'the act of learning' is thought-provoking. Thoughts are sharpened about basic themes, over and above the theme of learning, even if the subject of the day was 'the cuts in the county budget' and students' activities during a strike.

New strategies for school development

The study and the observations on the level of teaching and learning practice are pretty much seen from the IT class's and the learner's perspective. These together with interviews and conversations with students provide a proper basis for analysing the main theme of the CLASP-projects—namely, creative learning seen from a student perspective. But throughout the whole period there has also been a collaborative practice concerning discussion about school development. The school and the teachers from the IT classes still have learning strategies and IT based learning in focus but it is combined with reflections on strategies for school development.

In this sense *The Electronic School* project, and my fieldwork as well, are already influenced by the broader development perspective, dealing with new reforms and demands of modernisation and professionalisstion (Andersen and

8   With programmes for reforms of The Gymnasium starting 1999 and the new reform implemented 2005 as the broader context the school's own development work and strategies are described in a number of strategy papers and evaluative reports connected to IT classes e.g. Avedøre Gymnasium (2003).

Sommer, 2003, Hjort, 2004, Borgnakke and Raae, 2004, Rask Eriksen, 2005).[8] School development seen in the light of modernisation was also connected to evaluative research in the major educational development programme (Beck et al., 2003, Borgnakke, 2004a). Further more Ph.D. thesis and projects gave empirical analyses of traditional and new strategies for evaluation and assessment (Christensen, 2005, Krogh and Juul Jensen, 2003).

Empirical analysis on the political discourse and the process of professionalising and organisational development was given in Senger (2003) and Raae (2005).

To these projects covering the school organisational levels I can add a documentation project about project work and learning in the higher commercial and technical Gymnasium programme. School case studies with observations and questionnaires were carried out and reported by Svejgaard et al. (2005). The report includes six cases of project work and shows how the course and patterns relate to the different practices.

Cases from all six schools show that the teachers need to develop more specific counselling and consultant functions in relation to the students' working and learning processes. Teacher intervention is needed in the process when the students are creating plans, products and reflections on the process. But intervention is also needed in relation to group dynamic dimensions and hereby related to social and psychological patterns in the project work.

According to the development of project pedagogy as a model and strategy for learning the school cases show how project work is interpreted in the tradition of teaching experience and the tradition derived from John Dewey (1902/90, 1910/91) expressed by the statement of *learning by doing* (Borgnakke, 2004c). In this way project pedagogy also involves issues such as those relating to practical problems and the students' abilities and qualifications. The students' problem oriented work is focussed on solutions and practical use. But this process does not necessarily produce the qualifications aimed at through the teaching activities.

Critical analyses and the late modern discourse of learning

The CLASP-projects use terms such as 'learning in practice', 'situated learning', 'project work and problem based learning' to describe their sites of creative learning. Like variations on a recurrent theme of *learning by doing*, the striking maxims of progressivism, the discourse and the newest reforms confirm that the maxim is still alive and has consequences for organisational and educational development.

The analysis of educational development concentrates on new learning strategies in terms of IT-based learning and project work. The analyses show how the learners provide and reflect the late modern variation of *learning by doing*.

On this empirical background the CLASP-projects became a part of the discussion of progressivism, critical theory and the new discourse of learning. The question was how to sharpen both critical theory and the analytic sense of practice when education as a critical force is being questioned: a myth or reality? The question was also how to grasp the dilemma in education and learning as a late modern challenge (Borgnakke (2002).

The dilemma and the challenges are in *An analytic view of The Gymnasium in late modernity* (Borgnakke, 2004a), shown as a part of the political discourse and the process of modernisation at the upper secondary level. Case studies show the consequences for the development of school management, teacher professionalism and interdisciplinary teacher teams. Action research and pedagogical experiments with assessment and project work show consequences seen from the perspective of learning.

The analytic shift between teaching and learning combines analysis of school development with research on (teacher) professionalising. The political discourse demands development work professionalised at all school levels. Critical analyses show the double binds and the conflicts between professionalising and de-professionalising, (Senger, 2003, Borgnakke and Raae, 2005). Ethnography in educational policy and practice and evaluative research shows the conflict on a practical level, (Borgnakke 1996, 2004b, 2005).

In terms of research strategies it became a matter of covering both the political and the practical levels—and covering the conflicts in between the levels. At this point my research strategies are developed as strategies deriving from the classic fieldwork and framework and strategies taken from the evaluative research. In the CLASP-projects I confirm that the main potential in the classic framework remains to cover a field of practice: (i) by mapping out the field from the political macro to micro levels; and (ii) by investigations of the social and cultural practice in the learning context. I add that the classic long term fieldwork has particular potential when the practical process of implementation and learning processes are under investigation. Having this potential in mind the strength in the intensive field study is that it is a focused study of a programme, a school or a practical development work. With this background we can recognise an exemplary answer to the question of how we can investigate the discourse of learning and the new larger scale strategies for school development.

References

Adrian, H. (1980) *tretten års erfaring... (Thirteen Years Experiences...)* 2. rapport fra Gymnasieundersøgelsen, København: Stougaard Jensen.

Andersen, S. and F.Sommer (eds) (2003) *Uddannelsesreformer og levende mennesker (Educational reforms and living people)*, Roskilde: Roskilde Universitetsforlag.

Beach, D. and Dovemark M. (2004) Perspectives on schooling and learning amongst pupils in present day schools: The commodity problem. Paper ECER, Crete.

Beck, S. m. fl. (2003) Udviklingstendenser i det almene gymnasium, Hæfte nr. 36 a og b, Uddannelsesstyrelsen.

Borgnakke, K. (1996) Pædagogisk feltforskning (bd. 1), Procesanalytisk metodologi (bd. 2) Educational Field research, *Process analytic Theory and Method*, vol 1-2, Danish University Press.

Borgnakke, K. (1998) Group work and learning processes—viewed practically and analytically, in Tøsse, S. (ed.) *Corporate and non formal learning. Adult education research in Nordic countries* Trondheim; Tapir Forlag.

Borgnakke (2000) The Ethnographic Turn—and the critical empirical turn as well, in Weber, K. (ed.), *Lifelong learning and experience*, Vol. 2, Roskilde University and The Danish Research Academy.

Borgnakke, K. (2002) Skærpelse af kritisk teori og analytisk sans for praksis (Sharpening critical theory and analytic sense of practice), *Nordic Educational Research, 22:* 195-214.

Borgnakke, K. (ed.) (2004a) Et analytisk blik på senmodernitetens gymnasium (An analytic view on The Gymnasium in late modernity). Gymnasiepædagogik 47, DIG, University of Southern Denmark.

Borgnakke, K. (2004b) Etnografiske studier i pædagogik og læring- en senmoderne udfordring. (Ethnography in pedagogy and learning—a late modern challenge), *(*An analytic view on The Gymnasium in late modernity) Borgnakke (ed.). Gymnasiepædagogik 47, DIG, University of Southern Denmark.

Borgnakke, K. (2004c) Ethnographic Studies and Analysis of a Recurrent Theme: 'learning by doing', Theme: Ethnography of Education in a European Educational Researcher Perspective, *European Educational Research Journal*, 3(3): 539-565

Borgnakke, K. (2005) Læringsdiskurser og praktikker, Akademisk Forlag.

Borgnakke, K. and Raae P. H. (2004) Professionaliseringsgevinsten—lærerprofessionalisering gennem forsøg og udviklingsarbejde, Professionsforskning i Danmark, K. Hjort (ed.) Roskilde Universitetsforlag.

Christensen, T. S. (2005) Integreret evaluering. (Integration of Assessment and Instruction—an Educational Experiment). Ph.d. thesis, DIG. Odense, University of Southern Denmark.

Dewey, J. (1902/90) *The School and Society. The Child and the Curriculum.* Chicago: The University of Chicago Press.

Dewey, J. (1910/91) *How We Think.* New York: Prometheus Books.

Dovemark, M. (2004) Responsibility, flexibility, freedom of choice: An ethnographic Study of a School in Transition. Göteborg, Acta Universitatis Gothoburgensis.

Eriksen, T. R. (ed) (2005) *Professionsidentitet i forandring (The Professional Identity in changing)*, Copenhagen: Akademisk forlag.

Hjort, K. (ed.) (2004*) De professionelle, Professionsforskning i Danmark (The professionals, research in professions in Denmark)*, Roskilde: Roskilde University Press.

Kupferberg, F. (1996) Kreativt kaos i projektarbejdet (Creative Chaos in Project Work). Aalborg: Aalborg Universitetsforlag.

Krogh, E. and M. Juul Jensen (2003) Portfolioevaluering. Gymnasiepædagogik 40. Odense: Dansk Institut for Gymnasiepædagogik, Syddansk Universitet.

Langager, S. (1994) *KaosPiloterne—evalueringsrapport Hold 1 1991-93 (ChaosPilots-evaluation report)*. Pædagogisk-psykologisk publikationsserie, PPP 89, København, Danmarks Lærerhøjskole.

Negt, O. (1971) *Soziologische Phantasie und exemplarisches Lernen*, Frankfurt am Main, Köln: Europäische Verlagsanstalt.

Olsen, J. B. (1992) Kreativ voksenindlæring (Creative adult learning). Aalborg, Aalborg Universitetscenter

Piaget, J. (1969) *Psychologie et and Pedagogie, Société Nouvelles des Édutions* Paris: Gonthier.

Raae, P. H. (2005) Trægghedens rationalitet (The Intertia of Rationality. The Upper Secondary School and the Changed Pressure for Change). Ph.d. thesis, DIG. Odense, University of Southern Denmark.

Rasmussen, P. (1998) Uddannelse og samfund, kritiske analyser (Education and Society—critical analyses), Aalborg: Aalborg Universitetsforlag.

Salling Olesen and Højgaard Jensen (eds) (1996) *Project Studies—a late modern university reform?* Roskilde University Press.

Senger, U. (2003) Organisatorisk læring og lærerprofessionalisme i gymnasiet. (Teacher Professionalism and Organizational Learning). Ph.d. thesis, DIG. Odense, University of Southern Denmark.

Vygotsky, L. (1982) *Tænkning og sprog, bd. 2 (Thought and language/*Cambridge 1962), Copenhagen: Reitzel.

Ziehe, T. and H. Stubenrauch (1982) *Plädoyer für ungewöhnliches Lernen*, Reinbek bei Hamburg: Rowohlt Taschenbücher.

Ziehe, T. (1987) *Det modernes indhold af irritation, Pædagogik and modernitet, (Pedagogy and modernity)* Bjerg (ed.) København: Hans Reitzels Forlag.

Is there an environment for the development of creativity in the project area of the basic education curriculum in Portugal?

Maria Odete Valente and Lucília Campos
Department of Education, School of Science, University of Lisbon

Creativity and its study became most important along with the development of science and technology and with the idea that difference has a place of privilege. There is an understanding that for a society to be free of stagnation and for the individual to attain his full development, every system of education must encourage the development of creativity. To research how some school contexts promote such an opportunity is the subject of this study.

Context

The project area in the basic education curriculum

Since 2001 (with three previous years of implementation on an experimental basis), the national curriculum for basic education in Portugal has included a curriculum area of nineteen minutes per week for the development of project work, known as *Área de Projecto* (AP).

AP's aims are project conceptualisation, realisation and evaluation, through the articulation of knowledge of different curriculum areas, around problems and teams for research or intervention, according to the students' needs and interests (number 3 of article 5 of Decree Law 6/2001). A certain freedom was guaranteed in the choice and organisation of activities without the pressure of achieving nationally defined competencies. Also freedom is empowered by the fact that there is no national examination until the end of basic education, and school evaluation of the project has only a qualitative qualification more connected to the singularity of each student performing his own work. In the classroom children's insatiable need for knowledge makes them rearrange their ideas into patterns that makes sense to them. Therefore, it is logical that the development of curricula should present creativity as an ideal of education. AP as an alternative curriculum area is, a way of developing autonomy, social and personal responsibility, the capacity to make decisions and the courage to assume risks as a way of developing creativity. Creativity is multifaceted but it must be stimulated, through a series of intelligences. Children do not have the same profile of intelligences and their intrinsic motivation arises from different interests. The knowledge explosion means choices must be made and the basic knowledge every student must have needs to be taught differently. Frustration and school failure can be reduced if teachers present information in different ways and offer students multiple options for success.

The Problem

The main objective of this study is to understand how the AP context promotes or creates potential opportunities for student creative expression and the development of their multiple intelligences. We also try to understand how it promotes the organisation of students' own processes of learning - a way of promoting the development of creativity.

More specifically, the study intends to answer the following questions:

+   How does the educational strategy of project work allow opportunities for creative expression?

+   How does student individual investment in school activities favour the development of creativity?

+   How do students and teachers think and feel about the potential of project work to generate a lived dynamic of learning?

+   Which strategies and activities stimulate multiple intelligences?

+   Which circumstances inhibit creative expression?

Methodology

In the study a qualitative and interpretative approach has been followed. Participant observation and the registration of notes have been selected as the main sources of collecting data.

The validity of ethnographic observation depends on a sufficient duration for observation *in situ* allowing the observer to see things, not only once, but also repeatedly. In the study observation went on every week throughout the year to allow us to follow the different phases of the work.

We also used some other ways of collecting data, namely the analyses of documents produced by students and teachers. We also interviewed students and teachers in order to get their perspectives about the work that was going on. The interviews were semi-structured and some of the questions emerged as the conversations went on, following a flexible scheme.

We observed twenty six project work periods for each class, during the observation. The observer maintained a note diary. For each class individual interviews were also done with teachers and students as well as one group interview with five students from each class. The document analyses was carried out simultaneously as teachers or students produced the documents.

The identity of the school and the names of the participants are protected through the anonymity of the reports.

Study participants

The school in the study is located in the city of Almada situated about fifteen kilometres from Lisbon. It is mainly a secondary school with an educational third cycle. It has about one thousand students during the day and five hundred at night. There are one hundred and fifty teachers and about sixty non-teaching personnel, most of them of an advanced age and in fragile health.

This school was selected due to the fact that the researcher was a teacher there. This situation facilitated the directing board's permission to perform the research and develop contact with the teachers of the different classes as well as with the students of the study.

The classes observed were one of the 7th grade and two of the 8th grade classes. The observation took place from September to June during the academic year 2003/2004.

Each class has two teachers to facilitate the activities of AP. These teachers will be called teacher A and teacher B and the classes, Class 7th1 and Class 8th1 and 8th2. In 7th1 class teacher A designated A7th1 is also a teacher of Visual education and Plastic Arts, whereas teacher B of class 7th1, designated as B7th1, is also a teacher of Natural Science.

In the 8th grade the teacher A8th1 also teaches English and teacher B8th1 teaches Physical Sciences. As for 8th2, the teacher A8th2 is a teacher of geography and teacher B8th2 teaches Visual Education and Plastic Arts

Student activities during the academic year

The project developed in each class alongside an annual school project presented in a School Week and the details are indicated in the following table. In 2003-2004 the School Project had been the organisation of a Renaissance market. During the first term the students of class 7th1 decided to develop a solidarity project near an institution in the area where children and adolescents from 3 to 16 years old lived, mostly without parents or with parents without suitable conditions to take care of them. The students prepared and organised a social and festive meeting. They prepared games, a marionette theatre, and music and through different means they obtained gifts for the children. In the second term they prepared the Renaissance masks after having conducted the research, which would be used in the school project. In the third term they studied the theme of man and environment as part of developing their citizenship education. They selected sub themes and developed them with the help of additional teachers beside the project teachers. In the project curricular time they learned how to organise a Power Point presentation and prepared it.

Table 1   *'Area de Projecto' - School and Class Projects*

Classes	1st Term (Class project)	2nd Term (School project)	3rd Term (Class project)
7th 1	Solidarity Action in an youth institution.	Study and execution of Renaissance masks with re-utilised materials.	Learning to present a power point of the results of a thematic inquiry about ' Man and Environment'.
8th 1	Organisation of a class library.	Adaptation and staging of a drama *Romeo and Juliet*.	Learning and researching about how to realise and produce a film.
8th 2	Population Studies.	The organisation of some activities to have taken place in the Renaissance fair.	An Inquiry about sports and cultural characteristics of the Almada Municipality.

In the class 8th1 they organised a class library by borrowing books lent by students, teachers and parents and the resource centre of the school. They organised the requisition and maintenance of the library. They wrote reading notes in a file in English and presented their top ten most interesting books they read each month. At the end of the year the books were returned to their owners. The students of this class also organised study visits to two large libraries, The National Library and the Almada Library. The project of this class in the second term was part of the school project consisting of the adaptation and staging of *Romeo and Juliet* in English, which took place during the School Week, where the presentation of all the activities of the school project were concentrated. In the third term, they began studying how to make a film of the drama which they had performed previously. This last project didn't produce a film but only a prepared film script.

Students in class 8ᵗʰ 2 began the first term with a project of population studies namely: 'The Aging of the Population in Europe'; 'Decreasing childbirth.' The under population of certain regions'; 'Immigration'; and 'The lack of green spaces'. In the second term they organised for the fair, benches for selling Asiatic and African products, glossaries for the fair and a register for the visitors' comments. In the third term they investigated sports and culture in Almada and they carried out several inquiries about clubs, associations, sporting interests, symbols of the city and the presence of baroque style in the area.

Results

Having analysed the data, we present some results concerning the strategies used by the teachers of our study, the characteristics of creative teaching, the students' perspectives and we discuss the difficulties and limits of this kind of work.

Teachers' strategies towards creative teaching

Of all the wealth of ideas, actions, interactions, work, effort and discovery that characterise a classroom, we point to certain strategies teachers use that stand out amidst the data analysis and are important for characterising creative teaching. Firstly, there was an attempt to interact with every student in order to establish an affective relationship that is productive for the work itself. A teacher suggested in her interview.

> The teacher has a fundamental role. Of course we all know that each class is very different and while some are easier to work with, others are more difficult. To start with the teacher has to spend the first two months of the year trying to get to know the kids she has before her. We have to reach the students and not expect them to reach us. In order to work with them we have to get to know them and like them in the first place.   (Teacher A8ᵗʰ1)

We found that when the teacher understands that it is their responsibility to create the atmosphere of affection that is necessary for work, she invests the necessary time until she reaches it or;

> The teacher A8ᵗʰ1 plays, touches, kisses, scolds, calls for their attention, praises and criticises constructively.   (A. O.)

Her work as a teacher is fundamental in determining the classroom environment. I have never seen a lesson during which the class was so amused and motivated.   (Observer's Comment.)

The establishment of a class dynamic that suits the students' needs is essential.

I think it all has to do with the way the teacher is motivated and sensitive towards undertaking a form of teaching with her students that is really constructive, diverse and suits their needs. Perhaps it's best to say that AP is probably the reflection of the teacher standing before her.
(A8th1)

The observer comments on another observation in class 8th1.

All the students enter the classroom and start organising the space for the work they are developing. Those participating in the theatre play move the tables away and organise the chairs in a U-shape at the centre of the room. Those not rehearsing organise the tables so as to keep painting the scenarios. The teacher talks to a few students while the others organise the room according to the activity they are developing and according to their method of working. Some are sitting, others are standing, alone or accompanied. The students are the ones to establish the class dynamic they need to produce their work.   (Observer's Comm.)

The educational approach of project work constructs classes that adapt to a very wide scope of ideas, activities and a rich, diversified class dynamic. Knowledge of each student in terms of understanding his/her potential and difficulties is important for creative learning.

If you know the students well, you know their characteristics and you can guide them. That's what the teacher's there for ...   (B8th2)

While some talk about the class library, one student says to the teacher:
(8th2S): I don't like to read.
(A8th1): Then what do you like?

(8th2S): I like football.

(A8th1): Then let's go to the Resource Centre to look for a book about football that you like.

And they left for the Resource Centre. When they came back the student was carrying a book about football in his hand and he sat down, opened it and began to look at its contents. All the students in the room were now looking at the contents of different books.   (A. O.)

Knowing the potentialities and difficulties of each student allows the teacher to understand how the investment in each activity may be simple or difficult. Managing to do something in a situation which is hard for the student is a step towards his/her development in that area. Selection of projects based on the interests indicated by the students. One teacher states:

The kids will never work on something that is forced upon them. Depending on the class characteristics the teacher must choose several possible routes. Naturally we end up influencing them in the sense of what's best for them.   (A8th2)

Projects chosen by the students, based on the guidance their teacher provides, is the beginning of work that takes into account two important factors, the students liking what they are doing and the teacher being able to help in guiding the students' choices based on the experience and knowledge he has and can share with his students.

The organisation of working groups according to projects or activities was a major part of the strategy;

The development of team work is another strategy. Not only do they enrich themselves but they also enrich the other colleagues they have contact with. If they rotate in pair work and group work, I think that's beneficial at any age. Even in terms of autonomy, the sooner people come into contact with other personalities and with other people who have different experiences, other references, the more they will get out of it. They will improve and increase their knowledge and have a vaster view of what life is, of what people are about. I think that's beneficial.   (A7th1)

Or, as we can find in this observation of a lesson.

> Working groups are not defined from the beginning to last throughout
> of the project. There is a project, with several tasks, and the students
> carry these out as they emerge. Depending on the task, a working group
> is formed, when the task is finished the working group ends (dynamic
> working groups).   (A. O.)

Working forms thus usually consist of peer dynamics, group dynamics or the
production of tasks (without defined groups). This allows for a greater amount
of interaction among students, richer experiences and better conditions for the
development of multiple intelligences and creativity.

Discussion of the work to be undertaken was the next vital strategy. Project
preparation was both individual and collective.

> Each student suggested a problem to work on. After all the problems were
> written on the blackboard, B7th1 told the students to suggest strategies
> and activities they would like to do to solve the problem they preferred
> and also how that work would be presented. While B7th1 wrote the
> students' suggestions on the blackboard, A7th1 wrote them on paper so
> as to keep a record of this activity.   (A. O.)

It was also constituted by decision making and autonomy.

> Each group has a form to register the Project's phases. They have to
> fill in: What are we going to do? How are we going to do it? Who does
> it? How is it done? With which resources? How is it presented? Final
> evaluation?   (B8th2)

The answer to these questions allows the students to start executing the
project they had previously planned.

Self evaluation was used to assist the process and the teachers assisted the
development of a set of evaluation criteria, for/by the students and for/by the
teacher.

> Together, we are going to make a list of parameters to evaluate AP's
> classes. She writes on the board 'Cognitive domain/ Values and attitudes',

then explains each one of them 'regarding learning, diligence and execution/ regarding behaviour, respectively'. (A7ᵗʰ1)

Sharing was considered a major element and developed well being during their work in the class room.

In the multiple observations during the discussions about sharing, we highlight the attitudes that were shared in order to maintain the students' well-being during their work in the classroom.

> One student talks of the need for more tolerance with the other elements of the group and other students explain the need to understand, listen and help colleagues. Another student refers to the importance of being more serious about school. The teacher explains how important that is in AP work.   (A. O.)

The evolution of the development of the potentialities and difficulties of the students is such that by the third term they already have enough meaningful experiences to be able to think, create and manage the necessary means for the development of the project they are carrying out.

> In this last project in the third term they had the freedom to do as much research as they wanted on a particular sub-topic, organise and choose the information and produce the *PowerPoint* slides the way they wanted, with whatever content they wished. This autonomy allows them to be creative in terms of text, image and presentation.   (Interview B7ᵗʰ1)

Presentation of the final product was important although some teachers felt the process to be the priority

> It doesn't seem to be enough if there is no final product. Of course during the process they develop a lot of things, but I think reaching a final product is good, for their self-esteem. It might not be essential, but it's beneficial.   (Interview B7ᵗʰ1)

The presentation phase of the final product benefited the students despite the fact that teachers did not consider it as a fundamental phase.

The final product according to one teacher is, 'the icing on the cake'.
(Interview B7ᵗʰ1)

Accompanying each student according to his/her individual need is, however, the basis the development of autonomy

> It's fine to talk about autonomy, but they're children and the teacher's role is like the father's role at home, the father has to accompany his son until he is autonomous, and autonomy is something you acquire gradually, depending on your growth. Here it's the same thing. The autonomy I expect of my 7ᵗʰ grade students isn't the same as I expect from an 8ᵗʰ or 9ᵗʰ grader. There is always someone behind the development of autonomy. When birds begin to fly they do it alone, but their parents are always around and if need be they place themselves under them. Our role as teachers and educators is a bit like that: flying with them so no-one falls.   (Interview A8ᵗʰ1)

Characteristics of Creative Learning

The use of a project methodology in these classes attempts to create the conditions that allow students to bring forth their ideas and carry them through, with respect to every step of the project they are going to develop. This pedagogic practice, related to achieving a stimulating, constructive and welcoming classroom atmosphere, revealed creative learning.

Being innovative was essential.

> It was a citizenship class and we got school disrespect and it was really hard because there were no opinions, nothing was written about it. So we looked at what surrounded us, the lack of respect that we saw. We couldn't just go to the Internet or search in books. There were none, we had to create things ourselves.   (Interview S8ᵗʰ1)

Creative learning stimulates a sense of energy and purposefulness.

> Teacher Bᵗʰ2 walks into the room and two students come straight up to him asking for the key of the cupboard so they can start painting; other students go to the room next door to draw on scenario paper. The History

teacher entered and also starts working with them. Some students decide to go to the corridor where there is a large table and they begin to draw a map of the world. Colleagues from other classes passing by and wanting to help may do so. There's clearly a lot of energy and motivation too ... each one searches the best way to do his/her work   (A. O.).

It can also stimulate collaborative efforts.

Two groups had similar ideas and were working alone. They talked among themselves and reached the conclusion it would be more productive and interesting if they joined their efforts, so they decided to come together. They're excited about having made this decision. They join their efforts and it's easier to do the work. Therefore, S1 group (now with six elements) is going to gather toys and books to give the children. They placed a sign and a box at the school entrance and another near the students' bar announcing this activity and asking people to participate.   (A. O.).

At the same time, it encourages a critical analysis of the products. In response to a small questionnaire, one student declared.

The project I liked the most was with the play *Romeo and Juliet*, because it was lots of fun, we learned things like acting, and also because we presented the project to the school and it was a success.
(Documents S8[th]1)

During a 7[th]1 class some students referred to the products of their work as follows.

As for the masks they made, one student said he'd never made anything so ugly, another said his mask looked like *Spiderman's*. Some of the girls were happy with the masks they'd made, they put them on and laughed
(A. O.)

Evaluative reflections were informative.

> I like this year more than last year. Because last year we only did things
> we didn't know how to do. This year I'm better at choosing the activities
> I can do. It's easier now.   (Interview S 8[th]2)

Having different projects each year is good for them for they use the experience
they develop throughout the year. Using mistakes is part of that reflective
evaluation.

> During the rehearsal the students say the phrases in English wrongly.
> The teacher corrects the way they are pronouncing and reading. She
> doesn't criticise them at all, she just says the text correctly and asks them
> to repeat it until they say it well. The teacher also corrects the students'
> bodily expressions as they read attentively. The students are at ease, they
> laugh and try to do it as best they can until everything is OK (A. O.).

It is up to the teacher to help his students look upon their mistakes as a way
of learning a constructive perspective of knowledge and to develop personality.
To have the possibility of making a mistake, in a classroom, is a crucial factor
for the student to allow him/herself to be creative. A student who is afraid to
expose him/herself in a classroom may tend to undervalue his/her ideas and
abilities if teachers and colleagues are not receptive towards them.

> Personal development is also a feature of creative learning, 'before this
> theatre play I was shyer, now I'm not so much'. (Interview S 8[th]1) Another
> student stated: 'I never thought I could speak English as well as I did
> during the play. I was never good at speaking English, now I actually
> think I have a knack for it'.   (Interview S 8[th]1)

When a project is under way many difficulties occur that make it necessary to
innovative in a dynamic way, searching new routes and coming to some surprises.
The students used different intelligences.

> It was not just English that we could practice, but memorisation, the
> help from colleagues ... feeling at ease with one another, various things.
> (Interview S 8[th]1)

They used them in different circumstances and also at the same time.

During this project of Solidarity with a youth institution the students interviewed volunteers of the Food Bank Against Hunger, dramatised this interview in a puppet play they built, collected money through raffles to give to the institution and trained games and dances. They used many forms of intelligence throughout the development of this project

(Observer's Comm.).

The students give many examples about the way different types of intelligence are used and developed during AP classes. This type of project work values other intelligences besides those that are valued in curricular disciplines.

However creative learning also requires recognition from their peers and teachers.

S1 and S2 have already made the masks. They are really pretty and creative. S1 made two masks, one for the people and one for royalty. They are made of cardboard, sheets, sticks, feathers and cloth. A7[th]1 asks them to show them to the class. (A7[th]1).

Paying attention and valuing the student's abilities is one way to help him/her discover his/her creativity. The creative environment stimulates a collective well being.

The classroom environment has a pleasant, discrete noise. Everyone is working. I go over to the computer room, to the scenario paper room and also to the corridor. The environment is the same: everyone's working with autonomy, motivation and co-operation. One student is cutting a piece of cloth to make a waistcoat for another 8th grade colleague who is from another class and is going to be Sancho Pança. There is a sense of belonging, it is their work that they are doing with pride and motivation, and there is co-operation and solicitude. (A. O.)

As the teacher comments when entering an AP class: 'Wow! Now this is what I call real work!' (A8[th]2) The feeling of belonging to a given environment is necessary for student integration, without which there is little motivation for the development of his/her creativity. This feeling is supportive and allows a constructive manifestation of collegiality.

Feeling that there is space, time and colleagues available is manifest.

The methodology used in the class enabled the development of student autonomy (in the choice of topics and suggestions), creativity (in suggestions as to how to carry out work), respect for one another (all the suggestions were received without criticism). The teacher and colleagues express freedom and respect towards each student, so they may manifest themselves and, on the other hand, the student knows that his manifestations inside the classroom also have to correspond to what he wants from others. He must also give freedom and respect to his colleagues and his teacher.   (Observer's Comm.)

I think that before it was harder to work together because I had one opinion and the others had a different one but not anymore. Now I accept others' opinions more, I listen to them more and now we can 'show' our opinions to elaborate a better one. (Interview S 7th1)

Student perspectives

During AP classes the students experienced a creative type of teaching and consequently a creative type of learning, and this is understood in several references: they do not feel as if they are doing work, because it was not imposed on them, rather they projected it.

(S 8th 2): Sir, it would be interesting if we made a book for the people who come to the fair to sign and write down their comments.
(B8th2): How do you want the book to be?
(S 8th 2): It could be a book that looks like books of that time.
(B8th2): Then let's find information about how books looked like during the Renaissance period.
    The students left the classroom to look for the information they needed in the Resource Centre. They come back later with some photocopies they show the teacher. They are excited about executing an idea of their own.   (A. O.)

They felt it was closer to personal interests, 'it was a topic we were interested in and we took pleasure in doing the work, in searching' (Interview S 8th2). They had a more active participation.

'We do research, we choose, we organise. In the 7ᵗʰ grade we were given the basics, we were to choose, organise, construct a project and from then on we were capable of working alone. It's very good that we can decide and do things by ourselves. (Interview 8ᵗʰ2S)

Working in a group was a positive experience—they worked with colleagues in a harmony that was constantly being reconstructed;

To start with it's not just one opinion that counts, we have several opinions and we can discuss everyone's opinions. We can even join the opinions and find something better (Interview S7ᵗʰ1).

It was much more interesting to work on an idea with which they agreed, 'If it is a subject in which we can give our ideas and do things we want to do. There we can be creative' (Interview S 8ᵗʰ1).

The students are drawing the scenarios with the B8ᵗʰ2 teacher. Together they comment on the Renaissance images they brought along for inspiration. They keep talking until they reach agreement about what they are going to paint and how, then they start drawing the scenarios. They are concentrated and help one another. None of them wants the scenario to be badly made. (A. O.)

However, being creative also means working with organisation.

I think being organised is important for developing group work, you have to be organised, you have to help each other. I think it's very important. (Interview to 8ᵗʰ2S)

I also think AP made me grow a little in terms of organisation such as getting the group together over the weekend and doing work together. (Interview 7ᵗʰ1S)

The students appreciated learning different things.

I think it's even more interesting than the theatre play. It is just something else. For one we have to translate the whole text, which is hard work but we also developed our English. Previously we might not know certain words in the play in English, but now we really have to know them because it's going to be translated. And then as it's a film it's always different. It's a new experience.   (Interview 8th1S)

These classes are so varied, we did research on topics of Geography, History and now Radical Sports. I like to study different things.
(Interview 8th2S)

They valued being more open to the school and to the community.

I think it was quite important because we had to find solutions to the problem created, which was the production of a school week, I think it was very good that we collaborated.
(Interview 8th 2S)

I really liked the school week. I had fun with the suit I wore and I enjoyed bringing my parents here to the school to see the play *Romeo and Juliet* in which I had a role.   (Interview 8th1S)

However, they were not totally autonomous. They liked to feel that they had the teachers support when they need it.

I think that the teachers should support the students as much as possible because it is influential.   (Interview 7th1S).

We created a book with the help of the Art teacher. We really liked his help. He was always there for us, and it's what he's specialises in. He was always helping us.   (Interview 8th2S)

Creating an affective relationship with the teacher, whereby the latter is a friend whose authority, is accepted was significant.

"As the teacher shows the scenarios some applaud (when it's theirs) and others yell 'Uh' ... The teacher laughs with them and carried on without telling them to shut up" (A.O.). This expression of emotion is only possible when there is an atmosphere of affection, between teacher and students, and of an authority consented by the latter. The teacher shows no fear of not controlling the class because she knows she can count on her students' collaboration. On the other hand, every student has room to express himself because he has already given consent regarding the teacher's authority   (Observer's Comm.).

The lesson continues with no indiscipline whatsoever. Twenty-four students are enthusiastically working side by side with their teachers; painting the scenarios, and others take turns in rehearsing the play.
                                                                                    (A. O.)

If you like the subject but you don't like the teacher you end up putting the two together and then you don't like anything.   (Interview 8[th]1S).

Our relationship during classes also has a lot to do with the teacher's personality.   (Interview 8[th]1S)

Conclusion

In this study some aspects were revealed as limiting the atmosphere for a creative environment, such as lack of space for the concretisation of certain activities as well as insufficient material resources, including computers connected to the internet for their inquiries. This limited the dynamics of the learning adaptations of the student interests. This curricular area is supervised by two teachers, but the Ministry of Education has now decided that from this year only one teacher will be in charge of each class. This is going to limit the type of activities and the support of the teachers for the projects.

The most severe limitation was the education of the teachers who were not well adapted to the new strategies. Most had no creative experiences in their school years and in their university when doing their teacher preparation. Even the students revealed some difficulties when invited to be creative for the first time. Only with intentionality and perseverance throughout the curriculum will they will discover, and learn to develop, the potential of creative strategies and learn in a group how they can make products they enjoy and appreciate.

Bibliography

Caine, R. N. and Caine, G. (1991) *Teaching and the human brain*, Alexindria, VA: Association for Supervision and Curriculum Development.

Carper, J. (2000) *Your miracle brain*, New York: Harper Collins.

Craft, A. (2000) *Creativity across the primary curriculum: Framing and developing practice* (1st ed.) London and New York: Routledge.

Czikszentmihalyi, M. (1990) The domain of creativity, in Runco, M. A. and Albert, R. S. (eds.) *Theories of creativity*, Newbury Park, CA: Sage.

Eberle, R. F. (1977), *SCAMPER*, Buffalo, NY: DOK.

Gardner, H. (1993) *Creating minds*, New York: Basic Books.

Guilford, J. P. (1986) *Creative talents: Their nature, use and development*, Buffalo, NY: Bearly Ltd.

Isaksen, S. G. et al. (eds) (1993) *Nurturing and developing creativity: The emergence of a discipline* (1st ed.) Norwood: Ablex Publishing.

Jung, C. G. (1972) *The spirit in man, art, and literature*, Princeton, NJ: Princeton University Press.

Kappel, T. A. and Rubenstein, A. H. (1999) Creativity in design: The contribution of information, *IEEE Transactions in Engineering Management*, 46: 132-143.

King, B. J. and Pope, B. (1999) Creativity as a factor in psychological assessment and healthy psychological functioning, *Journal of Personality Assessment*, 72: 200-207.

Lucas, R. W. (2004) *The creative training idea book: Inspired tips and techniques for engaging and effective learning*, New York: AMACOM.

Kovac, T (1998). Creativity and pro social behavior. *Studia Psychologica, 40:* 326-330.

Livingston, J. A. (1999) Something old and something new: Love, creativity and the enduring relationship. *Bulletin of the Menniger Clinic* , 63(1): 40-52.

McDermott, C. (1999) *Beyond the silence*, Portsmouth, NH: Heinemann.

Michalko, M. (2001). *Cracking creativity: The secrets of creative genius,*Berkley, CA: Ten Speed Press.

Osborn, A. F. (1963) *Applied imagination* (3rd ed.) New York: Scribnerâs.

Perkins, D. N. (1988) Creativity and the quest for mechanism, in Sternberg, R. J. and Smith, E. E. (eds) *The psychology of human thought*, New York: Cambridge University Press.

Perkins, D. N. (1994) Creativity: Beyond the Darwinian paradigm, in Boden, M. A. (ed.) *Dimensions of Creativity*, Cambridge, MA: MIT Press.

Perrone, V. (1994) How to engage students in learning. *Educational Leadership* 51(5): 11-13.

Prince, G. (1968) The operational mechanism of synectics. *Journal of Creative Behavior,* 2: 1-13.

Runco, M. (1993) *Creativity as an educational objective for disadvantaged students*, Storrs, CT: National Research Center for on the Gifted and Talented.

Schlichter, C. (1986). Talents Unlimited: Applying the Multiple Talents approach in main -stream and gifted programs, in Renzulli J. S. (ed.) *Systems and models for developing programs for the gifted and talented*, Mansfield Center, CT: Creative Learning Press.

Slavkin, M. L. (2004) *Authentic learning: How learning about the brain can shape the development of students*, Toronto: Scarecrow Education.

Spindler, G. and Spindler, L. (1992) Cultural process and Ethnography: An anthropological perspective, in LeCompte, M., W. Millroy and J. Preissle (eds), *The Handbook of Qualitative Research in Education,* California: Academic Press

Sprenger, M. B. (2002) *Becoming a ãwizä at brain-based teaching,* Thousand Oaks, CA: Corwin Press, Inc.

Starko, A. J. (1995) *Creativity in the classroom: Schools of curious delight,* White Plains, NY: Longman Publishers.

Sternberg, R. J. (1990) *Metaphors of the mind: Conceptions of the nature of intelligence,* New York: Cambridge University Press.

Sternberg, R. J. (ed) (1999). *Handbook of creativity* (1ˢᵗ ed.), Cambridge: Cambridge University Press.

Sternberg, R. J. and Lubart, T. I. (1999) Buy low and sell high: An investment approach to creativity. *Current Directions in Psychological Science* , 1: 1-5.

Stevens G. and Burley, B. (1999) Creativity + business discipline = higher profits faster from new development. *Journal of Product Innovation and Management,* 16:55-468.

Tallal, P. (1999) *How new knowledge about the brain improves school learning* (Audiotape), Alexandria, VA: Association for Supervision and Curriculum Development.

Tierney, P. , Farmer, S. M. and Graen, G. B. (1999) An examination of leadership and employee creativity: The relevance of traits and relationships. *Personnel Psychology,* 52: 591-620.

Policies of creativity and practices of opposition: The social construction of student preferences for creativity in different forms of school-work within school classrooms

Dennis Beach

Borås University College and Göteborg University

Introduction

This chapter examines through one case-study how new policies for creative learning are 'developed' and or 'opposed' in modern schools and has been produced from combined work in two research projects. The first is an ethnographic case study of a school—Sci High—which was sponsored by the Swedish National Schools Agency between 1998 and 2000 to research the reform of the Upper-Secondary School curriculum in 1994 and the 1995 School Development Agreement (see also Beach, 1999a, b, d, 2001, 2003a, b). This project comprised participant observation in the named school over one full academic year, and sporadic observations and interviews there and in two other schools during the subsequent year. The second project is the CLASP (Creative Learning and Student's Perspectives) project. In this research, data and analyses emanating from the Sci High investigation were re-analysed in relation to CLASP aims and then re-examined in a new case study school (called New School). Field interviews with teachers and students at New School, who have also been able to read and comment on 'anonymous' edited field-note extracts and see photographs and artefacts from the Sci High study, have been important in this re-examination, but some 60 hours of new, short term, small-scale classroom observations have also been made.

A space-time dimension is the focus in the present chapter, from the total material produced. It is based on Giddens' (1984: 119) ideas about regionalisation (the zoning of time-space in relation to routinised practices), the ways demarcated areas are established in institutional places and practices that create and stabilise subject positions and identity possibilities and (thereafter) influence symbolic meaning construction and value formation (see also Beach, 1995, 1997, 2000; Gordon et al., 2000; Gordon and Holland, 2003). Space-use patterns have been identified from this theoretical basis in respect to creativity possibilities and student experiences in the education contexts studied.

As also Bengtsson has expressed it (2003; but see also Beach, 1995, 1997; Janne, 1908; Levy Strauss, 1967; Österberg, 1985; Pred, 1990; Giddens, 1984; Schutz, 1973), the human being is a *spatial and embodied* subject not a neutral, unreflective, passive object and space, is therefore, never just distant, extended and topographical. It is always dependent on human subjects constituting and inhabiting it (also Lave, 1988), and this is also demonstrated in the chapter.

Lived space is the term Bengtsson used to describe his intertwined understanding of space although 'setting' is a term more often used in ethnography (Lave, 1988). However, both expressions unite life and space to ensure that the irreducibility of space to only mental and internal (subjective) representations on the one hand or mere external, physical properties, on the other. This understanding of space as physical, lived, inhabited and experienced (i.e. social, objective, durable *and* phenomenological; after Schutz, 1973) describes the characteristics which gives spaces their human potential. We consider, in this chapter the human potential for creativity and self-realisation in classroom spaces in an upper-secondary school education context in Sweden.

The organisation of space concerns: the distribution and use of artefacts and 'room'; the techniques that are exercised in the appropriation of 'room' and the social practices, of which these then become a reflexive part. It may (at least to a degree) account for why certain places are preferred by different people under differing circumstances (Beach, 2000; Gordon et al., 2000; Gordon and Holland, 2003). All rooms have natural phenomenological centres in relation to the human beings in them, and particular *moods* for these people (Bengtsson, op cit.). Experiences of them may vary with respect to the tasks performed, the enactments, who else is there, the time of day and the state of mind of the individuals themselves (Lave, 1988). Lived-space is, in this sense, not only dependent on external conditions, but also on the internal life of human beings. Their experience of the spatial arrangement of the life-world acts as a centre of co-ordination for their feelings about their lived situation (Schutz, 1973: 102; Gordon et al., 2000).

We constructed a map of teaching arenas for calculating spatial organisation and use of classroom time for the present investigation in order to identify differences comprised by the ethnography (figure 1). This map indicates specific 'regions of teaching' identified from the positioning of furniture and the mobility of bodies in space-time in classroom contexts in previous research (specifically Beach, 1995, 1997). These 'room-spaces' commonly comprised Pitch (a front 'display' region), Bench (from the front of the first row of desks to the back wall),

Boundary (an intermittent region between pitch and bench) and Pitch Periphery (the space at the side of the pitch toward the sidewall). These constructed spaces were set up and utilised differently by different teachers and students for classroom interaction in different subjects. There was also some variation across time within the practices of individual teachers.

Bengtsson (2003) has suggested classroom architecture all over the world seems to show the centrally focused geometrical orientation suggested in figure 1. He refers to the artist Peter Tillberg's painting of a classroom—Are you going to be profitable little friend?'[1]—as an illustration. This painting is ordered so that all the students in the room are seated in such a way that their eyes are turned towards the viewer of the painting, who is in turn 'situated' in the pitch area as the main attraction in the classroom. According to Beach (1997, 2000) and Bengtsson (op cit.), this reflects the architectural history of pedagogical material structures that feed off (and also 'support') the notion of learning as a teacher directed, front-on, top-down (power-centred), 'reproductive' practice. This 'classic portrayal' of spatial organisation in classrooms, which obstructs a free and creative use of spatial resources, reflects the data from the present investigation. We noted the following patterns:

1. Classrooms are generally both physically and socially regioned in ways similar to those depicted in Fig. 1. and Tillberg's painting.

Figure 1.   *Regions in teaching areas*

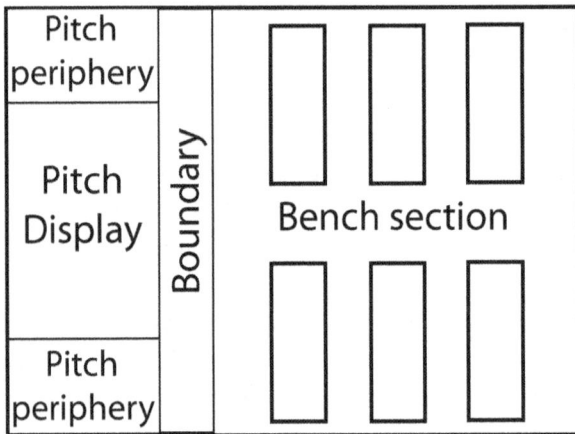

2. Teachers on the science programmes at Sci High and New School spend up to on average 90% of lesson time in the front spaces of the room (pitch) and that there is little chance of finding a student there in lesson time.
3. A few teachers worked differently to this. They spent less than 50% of lesson time in front spaces (particularly in Maths) and there was a good chance, in some instances, (not Maths) of finding a student there at some time during these lessons.
4. The same teachers teach differently in different proximities to major examinations. Different academic and practical school subjects constitute different settings and lived spaces.

The English and Swedish subjects are interesting areas of investigation in the present study due to their noted space-time use distinctions and because of this, these subjects are amongst the lessons focused on in the present chapter. A *general* plan that describes the English and Swedish classrooms, in which the science students were taught in Sci High and New School, is given below in Figure 2. This figure is very interesting, because the local school development plans and self-expressed objectives and commitments of agents at the two schools (teachers and managers primarily; see also Beach, 2004) pointed to an interest in open schooling and creative learning. I selected these schools after advice from my research colleagues because of their articulated commitments. The figure suggests that classroom architecture has not managed to evade a clearly demarcated (and traditional) pitch and bench regionalisation.

Fig. 2.   *Regions in teaching arenas.*

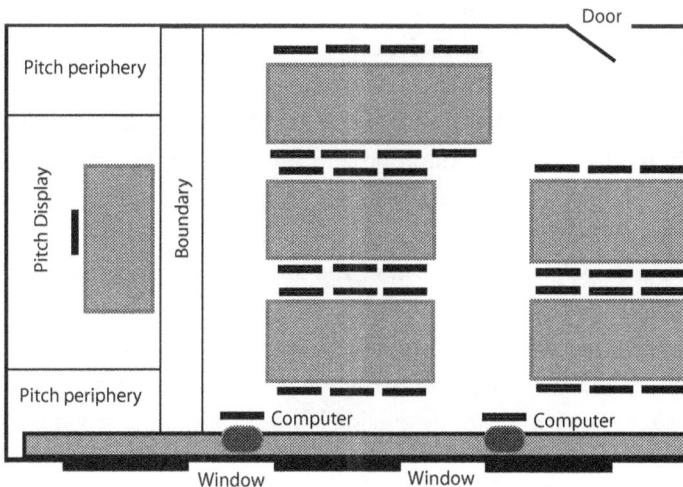

Space-time practices in and expressions about experiences of Swedish

Space use in Swedish in the main class at Sci High usually matched the kinds of power centred education described in Beach (1995; after Rogers, 1969). It was a transmissions logic based and formed around visible pedagogic practices with clear and concise rules to follow regarding the definition of learning intentions and how learning and examination activities were to be carried out. The following points, developed in line with Bernstein's (1975, 1990) notions of strongly classified and framed instruction, summarise the noted practices well.

1. The education context was one characterised by the reproduction of knowledge and ideology (rather than the production of 'new' knowledge). It comprised groups that were homogenous in terms of ability whose individuals tended often to exhibit competitive acts of knowledge acquisition.

2. There was a common *progression* to instruction, intensively guided by an assumed logical order of presentation in the 'official curriculum' versions of discipline content.

3. The pedagogic medium was characterised by a mutually appreciated (i. e. between teachers and students) social relation of superiority from tutor down to student. The tutor was the acknowledged expert and the student the self-confessed novice.

4. The characteristic *learning situation* comprised strong pacing and strict sequencing rules in two sites of learning: the lesson and the homework situation, made possible through textbooks and lecture note taking and instruction pace made it imperative. Learning in the two sites was regulated by strong framing characteristics controlled through decisions made by the teacher.

5. *Communication* between transmitters and receivers of knowledge was constituted by strong classification and framing. Time comprised a scarce resource and was 'treated', as such, by all parties. This strictly regulated the rules that shaped what was socially constituted and regarded as legitimate written and spoken texts, question and answer formats, social relations of production and discourse boundaries.

6. There was an *economy* of transmissions emphasis. Students were compacted into mass populated areas for instruction purposes and for most students as much time was spent learning outside of lesson time as in it and for some it was more.

The science students who engaged in the practices denoted above were generally (with some few exceptions) very positive about the learning they experienced, which might seem surprising given the lack of freedom to control their learning. Furthermore, they were also far more positive about Swedish classes than were their colleagues in a parallel class, where more open forms of pedagogy and 'freedom' were the norm.

Some of the main space-time characteristics of two classes are summarised in the tables below. These tables show that the teacher was generally occupying the pitch region in lessons with the main class and that students are normally in bench regions and rarely entered the pitch. However, in the parallel class, both students and teachers can be in places other than the ones suggested as normal by the conventional geometric classroom structures suggested by earlier figures and the reference to the Tillberg painting.

Table 1: Tutor use of space in 'standard' Swedish lessons (main class)

% Time in	Pitch	Periphery	Boundary	Bench
Lesson 1	96	02	02	00
Lesson 2	96	02	02	00
Lesson 3	80	04	07	09

Table 2: Tutor use of space in Swedish lessons (parallel class)

% Time in	Pitch	Periphery	Boundary	Bench
Lesson 1	36	08	25	29
Lesson 2	56	02	24	18
Lesson 3	46	08	20	24

The students tended to express more positive experiences of Swedish lessons in the main class compared to the parallel class. Common expressions were that they saw both 'a meaning and a purpose with their engagements' in the main class, which they also said they felt 'led to a distinct end-product'. Both these things were said to be lacking in the alternative classroom, where 'unclear demands', 'time-consuming activities' and 'little reward for the amount of effort put in' were forthcoming comments. The latter comment was common, which may reflects characteristics specific to the groups in question (which were described by teachers as 'elite-able', 'having a high-work-load' and being 'motivated' and 'needing to get on'). I put things as follows in my fieldwork diary.

> The (main class) students said that they 'learned something of value' and (were) more positive in their comments about Swedish than were parallel class student ... There is also symmetry between what the teacher says the students have done and what they (say) they have: i.e. 'acquired the knowledge and skills intended'. (And) the teacher expressed that he was very satisfied with the group ... They worked hard, (coped with) their high workload (and) were (one of) the best classes (he had met). As he put it, they were (motivated) and aware students who need good grades to go on to university on the best courses ... His job he said was to help them in this as best he could, which is also, what he tried to do. (Things) were different in the parallel class ... There the teacher described the students as unresponsive, conservative and difficult and the students described their experiences ... as involving poor teaching (flashy pedagogy) and wasted time...

There were two different kinds of lessons in Swedish; front-on teaching and student presentations. It is noteworthy that the teacher in the main class was very much involved in shaping lesson content (in both). This level of visibility and involvement differed extensively from the parallel class. The teacher rarely commented intensively and directly on student presentations and was usually far less visible as a central classroom figure.

Conversation materials with students from the main class, which aimed to get some kind of lead on their positive experiences of Swedish, address some of these issues. It is noteworthy that each extract begins by reference to the teacher and teaching (instructional aspects) not the learner and learning (constructive/creative aspects).

> He's a brilliant teacher ... He's very clear and has well-structured lessons. They are always, well almost (laugh), very interesting and helpful and he has a good sense of humour ... Above all he sets very clear requirements and sticks to these ... He's no softy but he is very fair. He works hard, even with student presentations ... For instance, a student presentation might not always be that great ... but he lifts it and helps us find a value (often) by pointing out what he or maybe one of us had noticed and then asking if someone else (had) as well ... I think we learn a lot in these lessons ... We know what he expects us to do and we can see that we have learnt something...

His normal work is usually quite brilliant I think ... as he is extremely knowledgeable and explains things well ... He motivates things and although sometimes the detail might be extreme (with) little room for us to shape things (and) it does go fast sometimes ... He explains really well and you can have a laugh ... You know how you are doing and he makes it very clear if he thinks your not working up to par ... The presentations can be nervous but if you are prepared, they're OK ... He gives us feedback and helps get a discussion going ...

He's a good teacher ... The combination of work is good ... His work is always clear, there are clear demands for us to fulfil and he sticks to them. He is very fair in this ... We get to learn presentation skills and practice them and we get feedback ... from him straight away ... Not just on the performance but also on the understanding we show and the effort he feels we've put in ... He's usually right even about that ... He seems to have a second sense about when you're coasting and when you're really trying ... It feels meaningful ...

The following pointers were regularly emphasised: clarity of instruction; good attention to detail; a high level of positive control and fairness. However, what also became clear, through the conversations with students, was that although the teaching was very instruction-like and could be expected to marginalise student interests and ownership of knowledge, creativity and self-realisation, the students indicated that 'they don't feel this'. They felt that there is a time for input, that they were able to express an opinion and that their own values were given space.

This is important from the perspective of lived-space-time and creative learning, for although the use of space-time in the main class might suggest alienation and the impossibility for students to valorise their own (personal) class-cultural labour power and values in ways conducive to creativity and self-realisation, lessons were not described in this way. Almost all Main-Class students stated clearly that they enjoy Swedish because they feel they learn something meaningful and when they offer something of value to these lessons, it is commented on and returned to them with interest by the teacher. Less than half of the parallel class students say these kinds of things about their lessons. In this sense, although the Main-Class students recognise that they don't steer the lessons, the tempo, or the content, and are not in any conventionally understood sense being creative in their learning they experience a valuable learning possibility not alienation. Their situation is one of being motivated students who want (and feel a need) to get on in the commodity context of a modern education system.

The term mutual instrumentalism springs to mind here as a possible analytic term in relation to the student comments (see also Ball, 2003; Pollard et al., 2000; Yeatman, 1994). Furthermore, although the students gave their own rationale for their beliefs and actions, mutual instrumentalism is not fully discountable even based on student terminology and their own personal descriptions of their education commitments, careers and identities. For instance:

> It's not reasonable for us to steer Swedish grammar or the history of Swedish literature ... Our opinions don't count for much there and rightly so ... This is just as it is and can't be changed ... He makes selections and (forms) content and he sets examinations (and) grades (and) that's how it should be (and) always has been ... in my experience ... We can have opinions about the texts though, how interesting they were, and what their characteristics are and so on ... That's fair enough ... The balance of freedom and control is very good ... Some things you simply have to know ... Others you can choose to do. Some things you can have an opinion on (but) some things you just have to learn ... He helps us get each in the right place ...

This particular tutor's intentions come together well with student expectations of learning within the settings of upper-secondary science education with science students. There is control and the strong classification and framing is accepted as supportive, of lived-value to the students and as appropriate (and responsive) to their experienced needs. Furthermore, these suggestions were close to their experiences of this pedagogy and similar to engagements with the 'softer' pedagogy of students' experiences from the parallel class. In the parallel class, where students chose more and had more freedom to negotiate content and form (i.e. be directly creative in their learning in) their education, the students felt that they 'weren't learning anything of real value'. The openness was false they said, 'because there is usually a correct answer to the things we study and a correct approach'. It was suggested that 'the task of the education ... is to show these (and) help us learn more effectively (what we need to)'. Students rarely blamed failures to learn and perform well in a subject area that has a teacher-centred context on the teacher's pedagogy.

Space-time practices in and expressions about experiences of English

Main Class English lessons at Sci High had regionalisation characteristics that were very different to those of their Swedish lessons. An open-door policy was in operation and interactions were more reminiscent of the invisible pedagogy (Bernstein 1975, 1990) described in relation to 'the parallel' Swedish class. In English the teacher's control of student work seemed more implicit than explicit as, rather than using direct instruction, the teacher tended to try to arrange contexts and content for learners to explore which were then re-arranged for and by themselves, in accordance with their own subjectively experienced interests. In this context learners' decisions about how to re-arrange substantive content and how learning should be framed (time-spatially) were important and students regulated their own movements and relationships as much or more than the teachers did. In line with the lowered emphasis upon transmission, evaluation criteria were also quite diffuse, and were often open to negotiation.

Details of the spatial characteristics of English teaching from data pertaining to the use of space-time are in the following table. These data support suggestions from field-notes and fieldwork diary extracts that students were almost free to come and go as they pleased in English, that they often worked outside classrooms during lessons and that they used the tutor as a kind consultant rather than instructor. These are characteristics of the classification and framing of education in the so-called 'new visionary schools' described by Dovemark (2004).

Table 3: Use of space in English for one tutor and three randomly selected students

% Time in	Pitch	Periphery	Boundary	Bench	Outside
Tutor	12	15	03	06	10
Student	04	06	02	75	13

The organisation of work above can be described as being resonant with the new curriculum ideals of a social constructivist curriculum and a socio-cultural view on learning and what Rogers (1969) describes as *person-centred education*. Work, constantly held open to the learner's ideas and creativity, is intended to help develop the learners' own thoughts and valorise their own personal knowledge. In this kind of context individual knowing is seen (and treated) as *constructed* on the basis of a reflexive fabrication fulfilled at an individual level through the development of individual and personal orientations to the world (also Beach, 1995, 1997, 2000).

The characteristics of English as seen through the present research is exemplified by showing and discussing student expressed experiences of how studying was organised based on an example of a study plan students were asked to make for their learning activities. An outline for study was agreed by the teacher and students at the beginning of term, based on national recommendations and was organised into a series of topic areas. At the beginning of each new topic, a specific work programme was written on the blackboard, which was then discussed, modified and then appropriated by students as a guide for further work.

The work programme usually comprised elements, like those described below, in which students were left to 'fill in details and ... form their own personal scheme of work ... for the topic area' (Teacher). Students were basically 'more or less free to use study periods, homework and other resources (as well as lesson time) to complete the work ... as they wished' (Teacher) and the teacher took 'a facilitator ... kind of role ... in that (he) was available for them to contact and ... talk with about the work and its content' (Teacher). The students had access to language labs, books, video and audio tapes and computers. An example of the written outline presented at the beginning of a theme on post-modernism is given below:

Read	Factory on Manhattan
Listen	Factory on Manhattan
Speak	Retell one part of the text to a partner
	Retell some facts about A. W. to a partner
Write	Describe a famous painting done by a famous artist
Grammar	Do 'Construction' and 'Do and Make' exercises
Vocab.	Glossary—synonyms and antonyms. App 30:14-16.

Directly after the completion of the two week work period there was a short word test, which comprised translations on words from the Manhattan text, and the students were requested by their teacher to write a few words of evaluation on their experience of using the study plan approach. This was typical for the assessment of the independent work done by the students. Both written and oral testing was used and evaluations of the activity from student's perspective were added. In each instance, the teacher wanted to know 'particularly whether they felt it had been a good way to organise their studies or not in the topic and in what way they felt it had been good or bad'. A table summarising responses for the work in question is shown below:

Advantages	Disadvantages

Freedom to choose/pace
We set the pace and choose
You decide on your own how fast you
   want to work
There is some freedom
It's a good thing that you can work at
   your own speed
	Time and planning
	It takes a lot of time to plan
	Time was short
	Needs more thought from teacher
	   about balance between time and
	   volume
	Can be time pressed

Structure and variation
It helps provide a focus and structure
Incorporates variation
The exercises were good
A good way to work because you
   practice different things
It had many sides that I liked
	Weakens classification
	(Our) emphases can be wrong
	I don't think it suits me because I put
	   everything off until the last minute
	I don't like planning
	Discipline is important and I don't have
	   much of that

Other Its good if you've got the time I think I learnt a lot	**Other** It was not much fun I think that this text was boring

Whilst the students had a lot of freedom in English to work as they felt appropriate, a general framework was still provided for the subject area for which the teacher was primarily responsible. Whilst students were able to experience some of the framing features of the education themselves, there were limits, which interestingly, were experienced most positively according to the above table. Comments from eight male and four female respondents[2] are used below to illustrate the main points suggested by this material. These comments point again to the same worries noted in relation to parallel class Swedish, about student concerns that they might not be able to satisfy performance requirements (examinations, tests, homework) effectively. These worries are related particularly

2   The sample reflects 50% of the class size and replicates its (65% M– 35% F) sex distributions.

to a public discourse about the need and use of standards in education 'which students have to measure up to' (also Beach, 2004).

> *Carl and Carl:* This way to study is a good thing to do sometimes, but not always. This time I didn't like to ... I don't know why. Maybe it's because the time was too short ... You (get) to choose and we can work as fast as we like without chaos. However, the time ... wasn't quite enough, because we had a lot to do ... We worry that maybe we didn't get what we needed to pass the exams (and) get the grades we need...

> *Sam:* The thing that was best was that we could choose what we would do and that we could write (about) the painting when we wanted. The re-tell thing was not that good ... It was quite hard to plan when we should retell the text and to whom. (But) I think we should keep this kind of study plan. It is a very good way to learn English ... providing you still get what you need for the exams and such like...

> *Lucy:* I think this is a very good way to work in. You decide on your own how fast you want to work, as long as you finish in time. There wasn't that much to do so it wasn't a problem to finish ... However sometimes it can be time-consuming in relation to the reward dimensions...

> *Henny and Lola:* It was quite a good way to work ... There were a lot of ways (variation) too. Writing, reading, listening ... But I think if I'd learned the words earlier I'd have understood the text better in the beginning. It's a good thing that you can work at your own speed. I think we should do this again. But not every time (and) the teacher should make sure we are learning the right things for exams ...

> *Dan:* (It's) ... OK ... not much fun, but I think I learnt a lot. I wouldn't want to do it all the time and I find it less taxing to study and work the way we do in Swedish, where the demands are clearer and where he gives us a clear indication of correct knowledge in the subject ... He stands up and tells and shows us what's right and wrong and he (the English teacher) could do the same too if he wanted to ... You're never really sure where he is if you need him ... He doesn't stand up at the front in the same way and tell you things in the same way ... There's a bit too much trial and error (in English) and it might not be effective I think ... But you do get to choose and plan the time more ... That's good...

Fred: I think it was a good thing to do and a very free way of working. And that's good. But when you have this freedom it's very important that you have discipline and I don't ... I hope we can keep on working in this way because I think it is sometimes a good way to learn ... But he should check we are learning the right things ... properly...

Tom: I think it is good but I don't think it suits me. Maybe because I put everything off until I just have to do it. The exercises were good but I don't like the planning.

Bob and Ken: (W)e should continue to work this way ... sometimes but not always ... This time it was ok and there were some frameworks but I would like a more tangible structure and more direct feedback of the kind we get in Swedish ... I would like this particularly when it comes to essential knowledge in English grammar for the exams...

This data indicates a lack of assurance regarding the exchange value of what is learned in person centred education and displays some of the tensions between the neo-liberalist 'choice' curriculum and the neo-conservative 'standards and values' one. As one student at New School put it, 'openness and negotiation for the less important subjects should not characterise the main subjects (which) should be more strict ... more controlled and determined ... more about thinking and doing the right thing than thinking creatively ... More about application than invention ... In other words, more about being controlled and disciplined than free and independently creative'.

These reflections suggest two things in particular. First, that the science students may have enjoyed an invisible pedagogic approach as a pleasant contrast in English because, as one of them put it, 'although it is an important subject English is not a main subject like maths that we constantly need to build further on'. Secondly, even in English new pedagogy fails to challenge seriously old structures and traditions with respect to the case of learner autonomy. There was an established framework, it was not possible for successful students to attain a positive subject identity simply through the valorisation of their own (personal) class-cultural labour power and values, as they could not step outside this framework and still be successful students and thirdly, they did not feel that this 'self-determined alternative' should be the case. The science students knew the limits of freedom and their potential costs and therefore preferred as much clarity as possible regarding what to learn and how to be effective, not the least because for the science students 'a real education (has) to be of value to (them) by providing good qualifications ... for further studies...' (Connie).

Time-space practices and learning experiences in General Science A

The *General Science A course* is a compulsory natural science course for all students in the upper-secondary school. I followed this course from start to finish with the group of Sci High students I have called Main Class and I discussed descriptions of the Sci High course with New School science students. The course was particularly interesting at Sci High, because of all the courses I followed in the investigation it was the one where spaces for creativity and self-realisation were most obvious, which is also, why the present chapter focuses on the course.

A 'map' of the science classroom used for General Science at Sci High is given below (Fig 3). In it the bench region was taken as the space from the prep-room doorway (in the left of the lab, 'below' the fume cupboards) up to the 'back' of the room and the pitch was calculated as the area around the teacher's desk at the front of the room. Boundaries and pitch peripheries were calculated, as previously, as the regions immediately surrounding the pitch area. However, there was also a back-stage region to the lab; the prep-room area. Normally 'this room is out of bounds for students' (Jen, Teacher) unless they have been given formal permission to enter. However, this was not the case here. There was almost constant traffic in and out of the prep-room and some student or other would be more likely to be in this room than the teacher at any given time. The darkroom wasn't used during my observations.

Fig. 3:   *The General Science laboratory at Sci High*

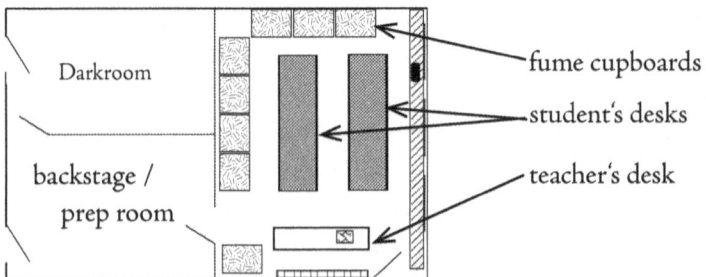

Invisible pedagogy, as discussed for the English and 'parallel' lessons in Swedish, also characterised General Science A, according to observation materials from participant observation, conversations with students and their teachers and observation protocol from structured observations. A table for space use is given below, based on the position of the tutor and three students (chosen at random from the class list) during three observed double periods involving practical, theory and student presentation sessions. As in the English lessons, the use of space-time is not geometrically standardised in a front-space/back-space relationship.

Table 4:   *Use of space in biology/general science lessons*

% Time in	Pitch	Periphery	Boundary	Bench	Backstage
Tutor / practical	12	05	13	60	10
Tutor /theory	22	20	08	50	00
Tutor /presentations	10	00	00	90	00
Student /practical	10	00	00	80	10
Student / theory	08	00	00	88	04
Student / presentations	14	06	02	75	03

The free use of available time-space resources in the Gen. Sci. course suggests the use of an open form of (person centred) pedagogy that is also supported by other observation and interview data. Students built up their course themselves around projects that comprised 'private' research, writing projects and laboratory activities that they chose and developed. Moreover, during these 'lessons', practical work, theory work and preparation for presentations (as well as some informal socialising) would usually be going on side by side. Students would be able to choose both how many and which labs they were going to do (between a minimum of four and up to eight—if they were aiming for a top grade—from a choice of ten) as well as how to represent these in their lab reports (pictures, writing, diagrams, drawings). Furthermore, 'public talk' by students was as common as tutor talk and a comparatively high amount of 'content focused classroom talk' from the teacher was traced back to student initiated speech events. Taken together these issues suggest two characteristics of the lessons in question. Firstly, there was no strict regionalisation of teacher space counter student space, rather students and teachers shared access and used all spaces fairly equally and secondly, public talk was also very evenly shared and reflected the presence of negotiation and co-construction in the curriculum, both of which are key elements of creativity in education (Jeffrey, 2003). These characteristics correlated with what teachers said about the aims of their lessons. For instance Jen, a general science teacher at Sci High, said:

(Y)our thinking (is what is) important ... You must use your own reflections about what (science) involves (and) devise your own approach and report. It ... is not about replicating known results and verifying established theory ... It is about thinking and acting independently and creatively ...

This is a very strong statement about the possibilities for valorising personal knowledge that represents a constructivist vista on learning, typical for person-centred education (e.g. Rogers, 1969) and is essential for self-regulated learning. This vista was strongly supported by the General Science teachers at Sci High and New School, who all expressed that they saw themselves 'as guides and resources for learners in projects that they (the learners) controlled ... in large part' (Ken). In their own terms they 'didn't want to ... determine the course ... but rather (hoped to) respond to students in a kind of living dialogue' (Ben). The Sci High teacher for Main Class expressed things as follows:

Unless we can communicate and create spaces for them to learn and develop their knowledge in, it doesn't matter what we do ... Their knowledge must count (more) than ours ... We must engage the students ... as people who (are) able to make use of the store of knowledge that has been built up over ... generations (and) we have to recognise the social context of the classroom and that the pre-existing ideas (they) bring ... are important building stones ... What they bring as well as what we do is important and they have to have the opportunity to develop their ideas ... I fully accept the constructivist way of organising learning ... Part of this ... means getting out of the way of their learning and freeing their potential to be creative and to learn out of interest ... This is an education project that includes their knowledge and allows them to participate on their own terms ...   (Jen)

These teacher ideals reflect the ideology of the new curriculum as expressed in policy texts (see also Dovemark, 2004 and Beach, 2004). However, the science students rejected their experiences of learning in general science almost out of hand, because they 'felt it infantilised them' (John) and provided 'an unrewarding learning experience (where) really nothing of real importance or new was learned' (Joan). This is paradoxical for the students were free to be creative and to determine the course of their learning as self-regulated subjects, yet at the same time, and despite the fact that they spontaneously expressed themselves as responsible young adults when asked about this, they totally rejected and denigrated this opportunity. Something within the lived cultural moment of education seems to obstruct the realisation of the expressed aims and intentions of self-determination, creativity and self-realisation in learning (as knowledge work) for science students in the upper-secondary school. I put this as follows.

> It seems that despite efforts (from teachers and the school) to create spaces for (creativity) strong forces and material requirements (grades mainly) push in the opposite direction ... These effects seem to stem from a performativity requirement and reflect the needs of performativity cultures ... The knowledge fabrication (creative and constructivist) moment of new policy and practices fits (uneasily) with older practices and traditions, like knowledge reproduction, correction (and) accumulation ... The old traditions (their artefacts and technologies in particular) still characterise the social practices of the school ... Three things stand out ... The conversion of value forms of education labour to an economic value form (i.e. grades and qualifications), the unequal accumulation of economic forms (and) the production of a normalising ideology for these processes.   (Field Note)

The ideas concerning the possibilities for creatively valorising personal knowledge in the curriculum were also tested at New School, in interviews in which students were asked what they feel about the kinds of learning described and they took up the following issues. Firstly, a subject with classification and framing arrangements conducive to and designed for self-determined learning and student creativity (in knowledge work) was 'unlike most other subject contexts ... particularly core and main character subjects like maths, Swedish and English' (Ned). They were foreign to the learning context of upper-secondary science as they knew and anticipated it, which 'is not and never can be a free space' (Lynn). This took us to a second issue, that being that the freedom offered in the subject was 'false ... because whatever happens, these spaces are squeezed very tightly by examinations (and the fact that) there are right answers anyway to everything we do here' (Ned). Students 'need to get good grades ... and the messing about with things in the way they do (in Gen. Sci.) make the demands unclear' (Evelyn).

Curriculum history supports the student beliefs. Formal education has over many years been 'governed' by an ideology of meritocracy in Sweden that is difficult to shift and that has been 'attained' through the valorisation of an upper and upper-middle class set of values, knowledge, knowledge-practices and pedagogical discourse (Beach, 1999a,b, 2001). As one New School student said:

> (Gen. Sci. at Sci High) doesn't seem like science ... There were no supervised labs ... Eventually they found a way but finding that was something that took a long time ... I don't think you can learn ... as effectively ... and this puts you at a disadvantage with those who do ... The Swedish lessons they had is good to compare with ... There they were told (what) was right ... and there was more assurance that what you were doing was relevant ... This is important ... We need good grades to get good jobs and good further education in the universities ... Competition for places is tough ... and what you do (i.e. how you perform) is important (as) grades decide the outcome ... or are supposed to ...   (Mike)

Feelings about 'security of investment' in education together with trust in the educator, seem to be of most importance for positive learning experiences for science students from student perspectives. These students have an ideological sympathy for front-on, power centred teaching and the geometrically focused, institutional material structures of conventional classrooms. They have an 'uncomforting worry (otherwise) about what you're doing not being good enough to get things right' (Karen). There is therefore a clear mismatch between the new curriculum epistemologies and recommendations. Constructivist and socio-cultural education idealism collides uncomfortably with the old (neo-conservative) epistemology of knowledge as fact and education as an examination of lived-practice.

Successful students make this point very clearly. Their preference for subjects other than Gen. Sci. comes from the fact that they feel they are 'being more rewarded' in these other subjects by getting a valuable 'truth package' that can be exchanged for good grades. 'In Swedish and Maths you get to know what's right (how) to be sure of this and how to get right answers' (Karen). You have an assurance about 'what's right ... and how good you are ... and this is very important for (your) future' (Carola).

Discussion

This chapter suggests how a resolution of opposing forces between self-determined and commoditised education is played out for a specific group of students and their teachers and suggests that these agents are in some ways conservative in what they see as central subjects, particularly with respect to examinations and grading requirements. Ambivalence was a strong student reaction to this situation concerning Gen. Sci. and parallel Swedish in particular, but (to a lesser degree) English. The science students at Sci High and New School rejected open pedagogy, particularly in what they saw as 'their key subject areas'.

> It was different and we were not sure how to respond to it.
> Adequate guidelines of what to do and how were lacking.
> We were unsure of what we were supposed to learn.
> We had to consult others about what to do and often finished up developing our work on the basis of what others did.
> We didn't know how much or how little time to put in.
> The work felt strangely uncomfortable, not like a real subject.
> It was like primary school. There was too little control from the teacher.

However, a rejection of the open/invisible pedagogy because of student conservativism is far too simplified an analysis. We must bear in mind when considering the rejections noted that science students are exposed to both artefacts (like textbooks and examination papers), technologies (like the examination and the standard lab) and social practices (of banking forms of commoditised education). These are resonant with a very conservative position and the cultural valorisation of upper and upper-middle-class values, knowledge and knowledge practices that has occurred in schools in (industrial and now post-industrial) capitalist societies over the past 100 years. Furthermore, they are constantly exposed to extensive forms of evaluation and have attained their present positions of formal advantage in school in comparison with their peers through their success in these in 'time-space practices'. In order to 'get on in the system' (Jenny) students are probably correct in being concerned to assure access to the classifications in a subject area that they are to be measured by, as this helps safeguard their accumulation of education capital. This is the reason why these successful students had gone to school previously and still go to school: see also Giota (2001) and Dovemark (2004) who have made similar remarks from research in other parts of the Swedish school system.

Two dimensions of antagonism are expressed in the chapter in education culture(s) supporting creativity and self-realisation in education. The first is that we cannot simply wish the history and traditions of culture and 'its' power centred pedagogy away and hope that personal, progressive values and professional commitments toward learner self-determination and creativity in the curriculum can then become telling factors with regard to education outcomes.

The second antagonistic dimension is that the realisation practices of alternative forms of pedagogical work are opposed by just about every possible and conceivable element of upper-secondary school pedagogy in 'mainstream (academic) areas' (including artefacts, techniques and social practices, history, architecture, social requirements and dominant educational discourses of performativity). This may be partly why alternative pedagogy is (only) experienced as OK and even fun, as long as it is restricted to the less central subjects, as long as important classifications of content are not adventured and as long as grades in key subjects can still be given on what is experienced as a fair and honest basis. It is in this sense that the interests of students that come to speak of classroom experiences are ideological and socially constructed. They are pre-constituted in relation to previous experiences and wider social relations and discourses that are themselves ideologically formed (Bernstein, 1990; Fairclough, 1989, 1995; Beach, 1997, 2000).

There are spaces available in which new ideas and practices can be constructed in schools at the present time, but these are limited by the past in terms of its relations to (and 'presence' within) the present. Both Sci High and New School were foundations for testing these almost Orwellian assumptions, as they were environments within which teachers expressed their support of the positive characteristics of a creative school, but where 'desires' were not sufficient alone to deny dominant discourses and ideologies of practice control over school education. Schools are part of a culture that demands comparisons and grading in order to meet the culturally characteristic necessity of differentiation and the ideological 'normalisation' of inequality. Schools therefore always evidence tensions in practice in the crossfire of performativity and creativity that go all the way down to epistemology (also Brosio, 1994).

The 'tensions' 'existing' between curriculum (expressed) aims and (actual) outcomes have also been identified by Cambone (1994) in a study of temporality in American public schools (Sundberg, 2003). Aims, like the ones discussed in the present chapter for disembodying the institutional order and life of the school, were investigated and where, as in the present case, the deep-seated differences between past traditions (that bear on into the future) and new vistas were not considered, and instead of policy realisation, signs of hybridisation were seen (Beach, 2001; Gustafsson, 2003). As Sundberg also suggests (p. 99), like Walter Benjamin's Angelus Novus, teachers and students were drawn into an accelerated flux of time while at the same time looking back and within this process new uncertainties were formed in everyday life.

The 'need of assurances in school' (Tom) is significant here and applies particularly to what the students studied in the present instance say are their most important subjects. In these subjects, the ideology of a banking form of education interpolates and students become afraid of not having done what they need to. Furthermore, although we may see this as an exaggerated fear, this collision of visible and invisible pedagogies (or performativity and self-regulation) intensifies an already existing dilemma between 'collective self-direction' and 'self-control'. What is signalled most clearly is that the discourse of self-directed and creative learning and self-realisation provides a poor vocabulary for change as, whilst it offers rhetoric of valorisation for personal, class-cultural forms of (educational) labour power, it unsuccessfully challenges the previously highly structured time-space paths of a dominant institutional order. Bourdieu and Passeron (1977) wrote that the conditions of possibility for any given form of pedagogical praxis are ideologically inscribed in the structures of the communicative situation and must carry recognition principles for their legitimation. In the present instance in 'prestige programmes' in 'good schools', education is still about the valorisation of 'higher' forms of class-cultural labour power, knowledge and values and success in this venture still requires self-denial and obedience/discipline (not creativity and self-realisation) from its students.

The present chapter, through recognising the necessity of self-denial as a precondition for education success, invokes a new understanding of the nature of a positive subject identity in education. Identity becomes an issue of the articulations of a social power and its anchorage in the body of a population as a material embodiment of 'culture' and 'value' at the point at which the codes of difference and distinction (often of the dead and their ghosts) of 'high-culture' are inscribed on the living, inside their particular and concrete populations. However, this leaves a serious question as to the real possibilities for new forms of creativity in learning as examples of 'integrated theory-practice artistry' in modern schools. Creativity and self-realisation in learning become issues of how participation is distributed as part of a structure of belonging within the particularly sutured domains of schooling (ibid; Beach, 1997b, 1999a, b, 2000). This is less of a question of subjectivity, intention and desire than it is of material history, culture, politics and ideology/discourse. There are also implications here for understandings of education agency, which becomes a material, political and ideological problem and the constituting mark of an abode not, as is usually assumed, simply an epistemological and subjective question (Fairclough, 1989). Even at positively selected sites like Sci High and New School geometrically regulated time-spaces remained salient in use in 'modern' (neo-conservative) subject areas because they are about valorising the impersonal knowledge of the upper and upper-middle-class social inheritance and it is still this that is materially rewarded. We are looking in this sense at a deeply alienated condition and at the way in which, as expressed by Marx in the 18th Brumaire, the weight of material history and inheritance bears down our best intentions and may also confound our intentions *in practice* (Cole, 2003).

Conclusions

The framing of time and space in the modern school has been described previously as monotemporal and linear, as a metronome that secured the uniformity of learning and provided a clear distinction between school time and free time (Gordon, Holland and Lahelma 2000; Sundberg, 2003). The new regime of flexibility implies a multitemporal organisation and the diversification of time-space paths (Hargreaves 1994; Sundberg, op cit; Gordon, Holland and Lahelma, 2000) through which a bureaucratic structure and its rationalised way of looking at time and space are transformed. However, what is actually seen when we approach school practices ethno-graphically is how these things are undermined by the institutional grammar of the school as an arena for a commodity form of education framed within a neo-conservative past that has been extended into the present and future. This is a problem of culture, representation, identity and repression. The construction (and regionalisation) of space-time in classrooms in the past has created an arena that reduces the complexity of natural spaces to the level of a physical, geometrical space-time surface for particular (truth finding) reasons in a way that is dysfunctional in relation to the goals of creative learning and self-realisation in the curriculum. This is why the classroom still tends to be more easily able to discipline its most successful students to be passive, uncritical consuming citizens rather than critically reflective and self-determined ones. It suggests that schooling must be radically rethought as an education of the senses; including those of criticism and creativity to help illuminate (again) what education really means and how it can be humanly constituted and reconstructed (Beach, 1999c). As Bengtsson suggested (2003) this might have been what Peter Tillberg had in mind with his painting: Are you going to be profitable little friend? It shows also that the present effort to restructure schools by reforming the curriculum is far from sufficient.

References

Ball, S. J. (2003) The teacher's soul and the terrors of performativity. *Journal of Education Policy*, (18)2: 215-228.

Beach, D. (1995) Making sense of the problem of change: an ethnographic study of a teacher education reform, (Göteborg Studies in Educational Sciences 100). Göteborg: Acta Universitatis Gothoburgensis.

Beach, D. (1997) *Symbolic control and power relay: Learning in higher professional education*, (Göteborg Studies in Educational Sciences 119). Göteborg: Acta Universitatis Gothoburgensis.

Beach, D. (1999a) Matematikens politik och ideologi. *Nämnaren*, 26: 56-60.

Beach, D. (1999b) Om demokrati, reproduktion och förnyelse i dagens gymnasieskola, *Pedagogisk forskning i Sverige*, 4: 349 365.

Beach, D. (1999c) Alienation and Fetish in Science Education, *Scandinavian Journal of Education Research*, 43(2): 157-172.

Beach, D. (1999d) The problems of education change: From the ruins of progressive education. *Scandinavian Journal of Education Research*, 43(3): 231-247.

Beach, D. (2000) Continuing problems of teacher education reform, *Scandinavian Journal of Education Research*, 44(3): 275 291.

Beach, D. (2001) Alienation, Reproduction and Fetish in Swedish Education, in Walford, G. (ed.) *Ethnography and Education Policy*, Studies in Education Ethnography Volume 4, Amsterdam, London and New York: Elsevier.

Beach, D. (2003a) The politics, policy and ideology of school mathematics, in Walford, G. (ed.) *Investigating Educational Policy through Ethnography*, Studies in Education Ethnography Volume 8, Amsterdam, London and New York: Elsevier.

Beach, D. (2003b) Mathematics goes to market, in Beach, D., Gordon, T. and Lahelma, E. (eds) *Democratic Education Ethnographic Challenges*, London: Tufnell Press.

Beach, D. (2004) Labs and the quality of learning in school science, in Troman, G.,Jeffrey, B. and Walford, G. (eds) *Identity, Agency and Social Institutions in Educational Ethnography,* Studies in Educational Ethnography. Volume 10. Oxford: Jai Press.

Bengtsson, J. (2003) Formation of space in the classroom. Paper presented at the ECER-conference in Hamburg 17-20 September 2003, section number 13, Philosophy of Education.

Bernstein, B. (1975) *Class, Codes and Control Vol. 3: Towards a Theory of Educational Transmissions,* London: Routledge and Kegan Paul.

Bernstein, B (1990) *Class, codes and control, Vol. 4: The structuring of pedagogic discourse,* London: Routledge.

Bourdieu, P. and Passeron, J-C. (1977) *Reproduction in Education, Society and Culture,* London: Sage.

Brosio, R. (1994) *A Radical Democratic Critique of Capitalist Education,* New York: Peter Lang.

Cambone. P. (1994) The multiple meaning of time for teachers, in Cambone, P. *Time for teachers in school restructuring,* www.ed.gov./pubs/

Cole, M. (2003) Might It Be in the Practice that It Fails to Succeed? A Marxist Critique of Claims for Postmodernism and Poststructuralism as Forces for Social Change and Social Justice, *British Journal of Sociology of Education,* 24(4): 487-500

Dovemark, M. (2004) Ansvar-flexibilitet-valfrihet. En etnografisk studie om en skola i förändring (Gothenburg Studies in Educational Sciences 223). Göteborg: Acta Universitatis Gothoburgensis.

Fairclough, N. (1989) *Language and Power,* London: Longman.

Fairclough, N. (1995) *Critical Discourse Analysis,* London: Longman.

Giddens, A. (1984). *The Constitution of Society: Outline of the Theory of Structuration,* Berkeley: University of California Press.

Giota, J. (2001) Adolescents'Perceptions of School and Reasons for Learning. (Göteborg: Studies in Educational Sciences 147). Göteborg: Acta Universitatis Gothoburgensis.

Gordon, T., Holland, J. and Lahelma, E. (2000) *Making Spaces: Citizenship and Difference in Schools,* London: Macmillan and New York: St. Martin's Press.

Gordon, T. and Holland, J. (2003) The construction of citizenship and difference in schools, in Beach, D., Gordon, T. and Lahelma, E. (eds) *Democratic Education Ethnographic Challenges.* London: Tufnell Press.

Gustafsson, J. (2003) Integration som text, diskursiv och social praktik. En policyetnografisk fallstudie av mötet mellan skolan och förskoleklassen. Göteborg: ACTA.

Hargreaves, A. (1994) *Changing Teachers, Changing Times- teacher's work and culture in the postmodern age,* London: Cassell

Janne, H. (1908) *See Le systéme social: Essai de théorie général Henri Janne,* Bruxelles: Janne, H. (1968).

Jeffrey, B. (2003) 'Countering student instrumentalism: A creative response', *British Journal of Educational Research,* 29(4): 489-504.

Lave, J. (1988) *Cognition in Practice: Mind, Mathematics and Culture in Everyday Life,* Cambridge: Cambridge University Press.

Levy Strauss, C. (1963/1977) *Structural Anthropology* 1, Harmondsworth: Peregrine.

Pred, A. R. (1990) *Making Histrories and Constructing Human Geographies: The Local Transformation of Practice, Power Relations and Consciousness,* Boulder: Westview.

Pollard, A., Triggs, P., with, Broadfoot, P., McNess, E., and Osborn, M. (2000) *What pupils say: Changing policy and practice in primary education,* London: Continuum.

Rogers, C. R. (1969) *Freedom to Learn,* Columbus: Merril.

Schutz, A. (1973) *The Structures of the Life-world,* Evanston: North-western University Press.

Sundberg, D. (2003) The politics of time in educational restructuring, in Beach, D., Gordon, T. and Lahelma, E. (eds) *Democratic Education Ethnographic Challenges,* London: Tufnell Press.

Yeatman, A. (1994) *Postmodern revisionings of the political,* New York: Routledge.

Österberg, D. (1985). Materiell och praxis, in Andersson, Johansson, Nilsson and Österberg (eds), *Mellan människor och ting.* Göteborg: Korpen.

Creativity in the Polish context: ethnographic research in the CLASP project

Renata Figlewicz, Dorota Wodnicka and Pawel Ciołkiewicz
Academy of Humanities and Economics in Łódź, Poland

Introduction

From the first CLASP meeting we were aware that creativity in the context of higher education studies can mean something completely different from creativity in school situations or in the kindergarten. We found, in the Polish literature on creativity, the following definitions.

> Creativity is a feature of potential creation possibilities, potential but not yet discovered.

> Creativity is an ability to show psychological transformation—a progress important for the individual and from society's point of view; a kind of micro creation.

> Creativity is an everyday creativity, a formation that does not always have an influence, but that is important from the individual's point of view.

> Creativity is a complex phenomenon (person, process, product, environment—3P+E).

Those definitions were the starting points for designing a survey on the interactions within a group. Our survey focused on observation and analysis of creativity processes, educational process. We assumed that observed process would result in a product and a form that was new and precious, that was important from the individual and group's point of view.

The aims of the survey were to:

1. analyse the basic associations connected with creative learning;
2. reconstruct a vision of creative learning, starting from its visible characteristics;
3. analyse the environmental influence for the dissemination of creative learning (detecting the favourable elements and moderations of creative

learning); and

4.   define the roles of all the actors in creative learning (teachers, learners, researchers).

The research questions (research problems) were:

1.   Is it possible to define teacher strategies as characteristics of creative learning?

2.   Is it possible to reconstruct this process to become more creative on the basis of teachers' statements and discussion?

3.   Can you define the roles of particular actors and beneficiaries of the creative learning process?

4.   Does creative learning depend on students and teachers? and

5.   What role does the teacher play in the learning process?

The survey was conducted with three different groups of students.

1.   The branch of AHE Konin first year of full-time studies of Management and Marketing studying the 'Basis of Management'. The age of students was between 20-23 years. The tutor was male.

2.   A group of students in second year Psychological Pedagogy studying 'Creative Activities' The tutor was female.

3.   A group of students in post-graduate studies, fifth year of studies Management and Marketing studying Strategic Management. The age of the students 24-25 years The lecturer was female.

Observation 1: Basis of management

Context

Place of observation: Konin,[1] Out-of-City Department of AHE[2] in Konin.[3]

Group studied: First year students of Management and Marketing, full-time studies. 13 people, 3 men and 10 women aged 20-23.

Researchers: Renata Figlewicz, Dorota Wodnicka.

Dates of observation: 29 October 2003; 5,12,19,26 November 2003; 3, 10, 17 December 2003; 7,15 January 2004.

Thesis: The researcher as a catalyst for interactions between the teacher and students.

Class observations took place on a group of students in the first year of Management and Marketing during the 'Basis of Management' classes. The

1   A small town near Lodz.
2   Out-of-City Department of AHE in Konin was established in 2003
3   The population of Konin is 83.400; the town is 120 km away from Lodz.

classes took place in an Out-of-City Department of AHE in Konin. The students
have problems with access to literature there. There are no state academic centres
in Konin. The majority of the group were 22-23 year-old high school graduates.
The majority of the group were females. In the winter semester the students
were to cover the following classes' topics:

1.   The meaning of environment for the functioning of an organisation.
2.   Multidimensional conception of an organisation.
3.   Different aspects of the notion of management.
4.   Hierarchy of an organisation's objectives.
5.   Management functions according to Fayol—planning.
6.   Stages of the planning process: prognosis, programming, plan creation.
7.   Organisational process.
8.   Organisational structures from radial straight line conceptions to
     networks.
9.   The division of directors.
10. Styles of leadership.
11. Leadership roles according to Mintzberg.
12. Schools of management.

Fieldwork—Researcher intervention

We started the observation at the end of October. By then the students were
integrated to some extent. We ran a short interview with the lecturer about the
group which was to take part in the project, before the observations.

> They are very calm and inactive students, I do not know whether you'll
> be able to observe anything interesting here.   (Lecturer)

> The Doctor is concrete and very demanding; we eagerly listen to what
> he says; he is a specialist.   (Student).

We started to ask ourselves whether we would be able to achieve the goals of
our research project, in such group, however we decided to take the risk. The
first contact with the group showed the students to be even more withdrawn
than we expected. As the class went on they were aware of being assessed and
of us watching them. The culturally grounded conviction that they were being
judged paralysed their activity and they tried not to 'stand out,' preparing their
answers to questions very carefully. During the first session we noticed three

outstanding people, two males and a female. At the end of the class it was clear that there were several sub-groups with differing interests. Despite the attempts made by the lecturer the students could not be motivated. The questions he asked, referring to their experience, were left unanswered. At the end of the class the students breathed a sigh of relief.

The following session there was a buzz before the class started and the students recognised us in the corridor. They knew we would be observing them again but there were some smiles and greetings. We hoped that something more positive would happen. Unfortunately, they were still cautious and withdrawn again, just as the previous week. The following Wednesday the situation was the same.

For the following class we prepared a Focus Group Interview (FGI). We started by asking several questions concerning their feelings about the class in which they were taking part. We also invited the lecturer to take part in the FGI. The situation was completely new for him as he had not foreseen that such an element would be included. At the end of the FGI there were some shy attempts to establish a contact between the teacher and the students. At the end of the class he confessed that he had made a surprising observation.

> Your presence perhaps emboldened them a bit, they stopped being so withdrawn (passive).

We looked forward to the following week,Wednesday (26 Oct. 2003). Everybody was curious to see if anything had changed after the FGI common conversation. The lecturer started the class on the topic of 'Stages of the planning process: prognosis, programming, plan creation'. It could be read from the students faces that they must have been waiting for the class all week. The questions came thick and fast.

> *Marta:* Does it have anything to do with what we said during the last classes?
> *Lecturer (T):* Yes. (He explains the connection. Finishing, he asks the students a question about their experiences concerning the issues presented).
> *Student 1 (S1):* It is exactly like that in my company
> *S(2):* I do not work but I remember my father talking about a similar way of acting in his job.

And so it happened—an interaction between the lecturer and the students. The researchers drifted into the shadows and the actors in the teaching process did not pay any more attention to them. It was their teaching/learning process and they wanted to profit from it, regardless whether or not they were being watched. In the next class, they worked in groups on specific cases focusing on an organisation's environment —closer-distanced, general-specific. The classes were filmed.

Fieldwork—Student collaborations

The groups were created without external intervention. The students divided into groups according to the tables at which they sat. It was not arbitrary because they always sat close to their friends.

The first group (three females) worked on the following case.

> The 'Helena Hairdresser and Cosmetic Parlour' in Lowicz is run by Mr. and Mrs. Zielinski and employs five people. Mr. Zielinski is up to date with the hairdressing innovations and takes part in competitions where he perfects his technique. In both the hairdressing and cosmetic parlour the Zielinski's try to use the best 'ecological' products to encourage young, novelty-following people to become the customers. Currently, Mr. Zielinski is attending a pedagogic course as he needs the appropriate qualifications to be able to employ under-age apprentices.

The second group (two males and a female) work on the following case.

> Mr. Kluska opened a small grocery shop in an old part of town in 1997, and he collected the supplies himself, mostly from warehouses and the grocery market. He employs two sales assistants, one working with the groceries and the other in the off-licence stall opened a year ago when Mr. Kluska obtained, with a great deal of effort a license for selling alcohol. Since then the shop has been open until midnight. This caused protests from the inhabitants of the tenement house where the shop is located because of the poor behaviour of the clients. Additionally, Mr. Kluska has exceeded a certain level of sales that has forced him to purchase fiscal cash registers to comply with Inland Revenue rules. This annoys him as does being bothered by the Sanitary Epidemiological Station over his old refrigerator which is frequently out of order.

The third Group (three females) work on the following case, 'Accountancy *Bureau* Kris (civil partnership)'.

> The bureau was established by two lawyers, Mr. Bialek and Mr. Miecek. They both obtained the title of tax advisors which added to the company's prestige. They specialise in providing services for small companies where the owners do not employ an accountant for financial reasons but at the same time the difficulties of the law make it impossible for them to deal with financial matters themselves. Customers recommend the partnership as it offers, in comparison with other bureaus, not only 'mechanical' processing of data but also help at obtaining a bank loan and creating business plans. In exceptionally hard cases, numerous contacts in the lawyers' community allow the bureau to direct clients to an appropriate and reliable solicitor. The biggest problem for Mr. Bialek and Mr. Miecki is constructing a good computer programme to run the accountancy service for small companies, because the available programmes are either too demanding for the service required or have too few additional functions, such as a payments module or the possibility of creating different financial calculations.

The first team showed a of lack organisation in the collaboration. There was no outstanding leader, no one to lead the team. Attempts to 'push' responsibility on to others were visible. Finally, the girls agree to begin and start analysing the case and put down the negotiated solutions. Two people are moderately active while the third one does not participate in the discussion, only listening to it.

The second team organises the work immediately. It is divided among the two leaders and a secretary. The boys take on leadership, argue about the proposed solutions, the girl puts down the final solution when she is clearly told to and the final version is agreed on by the boys.

The third team has an outstanding leader who runs the meeting. The proposed solutions are written down by one person. All three girls take active part in the activity.

The lecturer tries to help the teams, tries to steer the activity in an appropriate direction, e.g. when the boys have trouble understanding each other. He does not, however, takes on the role of an authority figure but acts as a facilitator, giving the students the right to propose their own unconventional solutions.

The second group encounters a problem with which they cannot cope. They report on a lack of knowledge about an issue that is also a problem for the teacher. It turns out to be an issue which should have already been covered in different classes. The teacher tries to present, briefly, the "missing" issue and shortly after they are back at work.

The groups then have to plan a presentation to the rest of the class.

The first group (three girls) cannot agree on a speaker because neither wants to do it. There is a short disagreement between the two active participants; the third is obviously not taken into consideration as she was the least active during the work on the case. Finally one of the active girls, without much conviction, decides to present the group's solutions. She does it shyly in a hesitant voice. The case is solved properly, the girls managed to discover the company's attributes and the threats coming from the environment. The other groups join in the discussion but do not judge the solution or the way it was presented.

In the second group both boys are eager to present the case's solutions. One of them summarises the negotiated solutions and the other complements it and comments on certain aspects. The presentation is vivid and dynamic. The boys draw the rest of the group into the discussion.

Predictably it is the leader of the third group who presents the solutions. Their case was professionally solved and they produced a professionally presented solution. There was no discussion as the class finished. The teacher said good bye to the students. However, they leave discussing the cases they had worked on.

The following Wednesday we planned the next FGI. We sit in a circle: the students, the lecturer and ourselves. It is an important FGI for there are many aspects to discuss. The previous class was videotaped and at this session we are going to watch some extracts and talk about the student's feelings.

> The first and second group read their cases from the sheets of paper and the third group do not have the sheet so the leader briefly talks about their case.
>
> *Researchers:* What are your comments concerning the theoretical introduction? Too long? Too short?
>
> *(S1):* It was OK. Thanks to the analysis we did in previous lectures and the short summary provided before working on the cases we could easily get on with the assignment.
>
> *Researchers:* Was the theory directly useful in solving the tasks?
>
> *(S2):* Of course. I think it was very useful.

Researchers: In your opinion what should creative teaching and learning be based on?

(S3): Mostly on developing our understanding of what we learn, it should be focused on knowing what we have to learn and our understanding of it.

(S1): It should combine theory with practices such as learning from examples. Combining theory with practice is important. Taking only notes does not let you understanding much. Sometimes I do not even look at the notes and I remember the lesson because of the different examples from the last classes. I think I will know how to use that learning experience in my prospective job.

Researchers: When do you think your learning is most effective? While making notes, using your imagination, solving practical problems...?

(S2): I prefer practical tasks; that is when I benefit most from the classes.

Researchers: Do you use your own experiences in learning?

(S1): It is difficult because we have too little experience, we have not worked.

Researchers: But, for example, observations, or observing what surrounds you, doesn't it help you in learning, in connecting the events?

(S2): It is easier for me because I work, so I have encountered some of these notions and situations at work, experienced it.

Researchers: Do you share your experiences with others in classes?

(S3): Rather not.

Researchers: Would it not be easier for you if one of your the colleagues told you about some examples from their own practical experience?

(S1): Certainly it would be easier for us to remember. Certain issues would be associated with the person, the event.

Researchers: Do you think you cooperate with the lecturer in creating the classes, do you influence the course?

(S4): Yes, we influence it e.g. by asking questions.

Researchers: What are your initial strategies when confronted with a lack of knowledge?

(S1): To ask the teacher. I would not ask a colleague because he does not know either.

Researchers: Hasn't it occurred to you that you do not need help from the teacher, that you may not know certain issues but that perhaps you can solve the problem on your own somehow.

(S5): No, it would be impossible.

Researchers: What do you do in a situation when you're at home, studying on your own?

(S1): We look in the handbooks.

Researchers: Did working in a group result in you wanting to act strategically to organise your work?

(S2): No, we started out spontaneously.

Researchers: Was the work divided between you?

(S3): We started doing what we felt competent at.

Researchers: What happened when you were presenting the cases' solutions? How did you feel?

(S4): We've never performed in front of a group, we felt stressed-out.

Researchers: Did the camera bother you?

(S5): To a minor extent. It was more the stress connected with performing in front of the group, the possibility of ridicule. It was our first time in such a group.

Researchers: Do you think three is a good number for group?

(S1): Yes. It's not too big, everyone can participate actively.

Researchers: Do you have any further suggestions for more effective learning?

(S3): I do not have common strategies; it depends on the context I'd rather study in the class because if I do not know something I can ask. It's worse to study at home.

Researchers: Do you think you can influence your own learning process?

(S5): Yes, we can broaden our knowledge.

Researchers: And during the classes?

(S1): No, not always.

Researchers: What could you gain if the classes were constructed the way you wanted and the methods used discussed with you? How would you benefit from such classes?

(S3): It could be interesting, but they'd have to have an introduction because we do not always know what the subject matter consists of.

Researchers: Could you and would you like to participate in designing such classes? To tell the teacher what your expectations are. Would it positively influence the teaching/learning process?

(S2): Sure, then we would be able to reply on some pictures, we would remember that this part of class was created also by us.

Researchers: What would happen if someone suggested to you before a class, 'Let's prepare a scenario for the classes, we have to learn this and this, do you think we should include anything else?' You would then jointly negotiate the class topics and when you agreed on the content, you would deal with methods of transmitting the content especially the difficult parts. If this were the case we would bring in the teacher as a resource.

(S1): It would be very beneficial to us because learning would be friendlier.

Researchers: Are there difficult aspects, difficult topics in these classes?

(S1): Yes, the schools of management. They are very difficult and very boring.

Researchers: Could you find a way of learning what you have to learn to bypass the terrible boredom?

(S3): I have an idea. I did not like history very much, but I found a way to learn it—I simply imagined all the battles, the soldiers, their struggle, the battlefield. So it was easier for me to memorise what it was all about, how the problem was solved; or, empathically, I wondered what the king was thinking, what he looked like, what problems he had and so I learned. I have a proposition: why do not we identify the problematic aspects of schools of management and present in some vivid way to our colleagues.

Researchers: Would you like that? [a question to the group]

(S1): Sure, we just do not have the materials.

Teacher (T) I'll supply you with the materials [the lecturer joins in the discussion]. There are three subjects, who wants to work on the first one?

Negotiating the pedagogy is under way, the lecturer enumerated sources of information for each task. The students took notes. As the class finishes the students surround the teacher to discuss with him the programme for the next class. They slowly walk out of the classroom. We talk to the teacher for a while:

"It is a good idea, because maybe this subject will be easier for them to access, it is a theoretical background — concrete and boring. I wonder if they will rise to the task".

Summary

The strategies of the lecturer and the students changed in the course of our observation. Both initially assumed the traditional role of students and a lecturer, the master in the teaching/learning process. The first FGI undermined the patterns existing in the classes. According to the lecturer the students became more open, more self-assured. They started to have expectations both towards the classes and the school's organisation. Culturally grounded conviction that the teacher is always right and the role of the learner is to listen, take notes and learn what they heard throughout the semester started to fall apart. Also the strategy of the academic lecturer, who thought of his obligations in a traditional way and realised them independently started to evolve. Thinking about achieving the programme objectives was replaced by reflections on how to teach, established cooperation with the students; they both focused on the same objectives in the end.

The exterior stimulus, the arrival of the researchers, evoked interaction and undermined the existing strategy. Seemingly accidental questions put forward in FGI caused reflections both of students and the lecturer. They started thinking how to do things differently. In the Polish secondary education system, students are not expected to ask questions or pose questions they are not asked by the teacher and they are not expected to propose their own solutions. The students of the first year of Management and Marketing in Konin arrived at their classes with just such a conviction. They did not realise that when they are the subject of the teaching and the teaching/learning process it is to their advantage. The lecturer found it difficult to invite the high school graduates to actively participate in the teaching/learning process. He did not think about the possibility of engaging them in the didactic process. Specific interventions by the researcher revealed the willingness for cooperation between the students who realised what kind of expectations they were allowed to have concerning the subject and the lecturer who needed their help did not know that he could ask for it and get it.

After the last FGI the students took the initiative. They prepared the next class. Each of the groups prepared their part of the material on the schools of management. And to the teacher's surprise they did well. These results were the effects of their ability to work unaided and cooperation with the lecturer. They were not afraid to express their own opinions; the teacher could always count on their critical remarks and he learnt the difficult parts of the material.

One more positive aspect of the researchers' intervention was the fact that both sides expressed a willingness to cooperate in designing the classes of the Bases of Management in the next semester. The experiences collected in the process with the audio and video materials will be the basis for the construction of the training materials for future researchers and academic teachers with the aim of disseminating the applied methodology to propagate Creative Learning and Student's Perspective.

Observation 2: Creative activities

Context

Place of observation: AHE

Group studied: first year students of Pedagogics, full-time studies. 28 people, 1 man and 24 women aged 20-23.

Researcher: Pawel Ciokiewicz

Dates of observation: 29 October 2003 5,12,19,26 November 2003 3, 10, 17 December 2003 7, 15 January 2004

Thesis: The student is the main actor in the education process. He/she acts creatively to ameliorate the constraints of meaningful learning. An academic teacher is a director in the didactic process. That is the reason why he has to observe his/her actors closely, learn from them and draw upon their potential.

Below we present a description of some chosen classes carried out during a course of Creative Activities at the Academy of Humanities and Economics. The classes took place during the winter semester in the academic year 2003/2004. There were 25 students in the group of students. It was their second year of psychological pedagogy.

The first of the classes concerned using a method of painting with fingers. The second class concerned analogies and metaphors and the third one focused on the consideration of the term 'Proteus'. The common idea of those classes was to encourage students to be creative in challenging the constraints and obstacles, characteristic of everyday life. Students were forced during the class to look at things from another point of view and to look at matters in a less familiar way.

1. Painting with fingers

The tutor brought specially prepared paint, which you can paint with using only your fingers. The introduction to the main part of the task was a short dialogue between the tutor and the participants. The tutor firstly wanted the participants to ask themselves three short questions. The point was to think for a moment and make up a question they would like to ask themselves. Then the students wrote the questions on pieces of paper. After a short while the tutor asked everyone to try and answer the questions. The point was not to read the questions and answers but to think about them and try to answer the questions for each other. The tutor asked if someone would like to present their thoughts, but nobody wanted to do that.

Then the tutor asked them to think about the difficulties of answering the questions. Participants had to think about the problem of actually answering the questions. Observing the reactions of the students, we recognised that the problems were new to them as we do not often think of these problems concerning questions in everyday life.

The next task was to choose one of the questions written down earlier. The tutor wanted the students to choose the most important one concerning them. While performing this task, the group was not very active. From time to time there were questions, 'And what if somebody does not want to ask question?', 'And what if someone knows all the answers?' These questions indicated a rather sceptical aptitude towards executing the tutor's requests. At the same time as the task went on their attitude was changing. The students became more open (especially when the main part of the task started, that is painting with the use of fingers).

After finishing this part of the class, the main task began. Firstly the tutor presented a short historical description of the finger painting method and gave the participants tips on the literature about the subject. The students got familiar with the history of the method, its first use, its purposes and benefits. After this short description the tutor asked the students to express themselves using the technique of painting with fingers. There was no additional description of the task or comments. After that the tutor and the participants started to prepare the room for painting. It was necessary to construct one big table in the middle of the room using the desks. Every participant received a large piece of paper, then they poured the paint into containers and coloured it with pigment. When everything was prepared, the painting began.

It is difficult to describe artistic works but this was not the aim of this study. Much more important was describing the process, in which the artistic works were created. In the following part of this description we present an attempt to characterise this process.

During the execution of the exercise the atmosphere was very casual and pleasant. Students presented a positive attitude towards this task. You could hear them express the opinion that it was an interesting method. Many people expressed their wish to use it on their own projects. The participants wanted to know the recipe for the paint and because of those questions, the tutor brought the recipe for making the paint to the next class.

At the beginning the researcher observed some distance and uncertainty. This mainly concerned the moment they had to put their fingers into the containers of paint. However, after the first contact with the paint, it appeared that this experience was deemed quite pleasant and there was nothing to fear. From that moment on the painting started.

The participants made comments on others' creations, asking what it was. The common table, around which everyone gathered, favoured direct communication, a constant exchange of comments, opinion and assessments. Students were walking around the table exchanging the jars with paint, looking for the suitable colours (the containers with paint were put around the table, so sometimes it was necessary to look for a particular colour in the other end of the room).

The time designated for painting passed very fast. The tutor let those who had not finished complete their pictures after the time allocated for the activity. In the meantime, those who completed the task washed their hands. Most of students thought that the class had finished and perhaps that was why the last part of the exercise difficult appeared difficult.

The last planned element was discussing the progress of the exercise and presenting the pictures. This part was only partly successful. Students were willing to answer the questions about the progress of the task and their impressions while painting and most of their opinions were very similar. Almost all of them claimed that this was a very interesting technique, that it allowed them to break some barriers and made the participants more open. Students were considerably less willing to talk about their pictures.

To sum up we can say that the students were very much involved in executing the exercise; they were almost all the time very active. Very often they talked to each other, asking questions of the tutor and communicating with each other.

The time provided for the class passed by very fast. In the end students expressed positive opinions about the conduct of the class.

2. Analogies and metaphors

This class was dedicated to analogies and metaphors, to show the students that in everyday life we all use those constructions. The objective of the class was firstly, to show how people's thinking is based on some kind of system and secondly, to reflect on how you can challenge these schemes. Of course, the aims were very ambitious and the realisation of these aims was not easy because it required a suspension of the usual way of regarding the world. We acknowledge that this class was much more difficult then the one described above. Before starting the description of running of the class we present a definition of analogy and metaphor from the dictionary.

> *Analogy* (gr. analogia = equal relation, equality) 1. Resemblance to things, situations, processes different from each other. 2. Logic: understanding through analogy is transposing the theorem about one subject into another subject on the basis of resemblance between them.
> *Metaphora* (gr. metaphora = transmission) stylistic figure based on such a connecting of words that at least one of them receives new meaning.

At the beginning the tutor asked the students: What does analogy mean and what is metaphor? How do they understand these conceptions? Other questions concerned some issues: What are the differences between the metaphor and the analogy? When do we use analogy, and metaphor? In which field can you use metaphor or analogy?

Student weren't willing to participate in the discussion at the beginning. There were only shy voices from the group. Metaphor mostly meant for the students, a way of explaining a thing 'as a short cut', metaphorical statements were more graphical. Students provided examples of using the metaphor in their everyday life but they mostly thought that you come across metaphor in the sphere of politics or in the church.

It is worth noticing that the students understanding of the difference between the metaphor and analogy was not always clear. To some extent those associations were considered rather synonymous. Metaphor was perceived more as a literary figure, present in literature rather than in everyday life.

The tutor then asked them to provide examples of analogies and metaphors that crossed student's minds in response to a word provided by the teacher. The first word the tutor said was 'school'. The task of the students was to express any metaphors or analogies they could think of. Below we present the examples.

Is like   (metaphor)

School—bench, desert, (it is dry)

School—book, shopping mall, (it is full of people)

Tables—forest, (open for everyone)

Institution

Teacher

Find an analogical object

Hive

Anthill

After an introduction, the students had to connect the words written by the tutor on the table

Child

Scientist

Firm

School

Director

City

Patient

Parliament

Television

Crowded bus

Matejko's painting

Village's household

Chocolate factory

Attractive woman

Shepherd

Mummy

Old newspaper

A Roman

Every student had to create pairs out of those words, for example; 'A child is like a chocolate factory, because it is so sweet'. After that, those who wished to read their sentences out to the group. Only a few did. Then they created stories about the sentences.

Picture 1. A young girl looking in the camera.

Picture 2. A lying lion.

Then every group had to read their ideas. Students did not want to do that willingly. Afterwards they had to rethink the story and find the anthologies and metaphor. It was not easy for them. Firstly they presented one of the stories. Photo 1.

> A girl in a park. A girl was walking through a park coming back home. She was tired after work. To rest, she decided to lean against a tree for a moment. The photographer took a picture of this moment, in which she appeared relaxed after a whole day of hard work.

Then they had to redefine the story once again and find metaphors in it, which was very difficult. Then they had to reinterpret a story:

> In this case the group did not interpret the relationship of nature to culture. Culture was represented by work and nature a source of force. The message was that a person meeting problems at work has to integrate with the nature.

Presenting the story and reinterpreting it was the last part of the task. Students did not want to talk about the exercise after finishing it but we think they realised how to use analogies and metaphors

3. Proteus

The tutor asked the students what they thought of when they heard about *Proteus*. They had to write on the paper their words. Those were examples:

> Distinctive person
> Weirdo
> Original
> Freak
> Other
> Someone alien
> Someone other then the rest
> Someone that does not fit into the situation

There were also associations concerning particular persons, mostly known from the media, for example Damian from Bar (a participant of one of the polish reality show programmes), Kuba Wojewódzki (mostly known from the programme *Idol*).

The next task was to create a vision of a *proteus*. For this purpose students were to use the coloured newspapers, glue, scissors and markers they brought. The order was to create a *proteus*. There were no other tips, comments or restrictions from the tutor. The only limit was the material they had and the imagination of the participants. The students had no restrictions concerning their vision of a *proteus*. The results were drawings, paper figures etc. Students had more or less forty five minutes for creating their vision of a *proteus*. And again, as was the case in the painting with ten fingers, it was not important to us what visions were created, but how they were created. The point was to reconstruct the process of creating an imagined vision of a *proteus*. The interactions between the students and between the tutor and students were much more important.

In this case students worked much more individually. Then the students had to comment on the pictures, showing the cards and writing their opinions on them. Next step was to answer the question, What can the *Proteus* do that you cannot? It was an attempt to change their point of view, because by defining 'Proteus' we were willing to associate our own vision with the vision of the rest of the students. Posing a question was an attempt to re-define the situation. There has to exist a situation in which we can negate a symmetry, *Proteus* has to be worse than us, it cannot be better in any way.

When the students started to talk about what *Proteus* could do and what it cannot it made think of limits — their limits. The tutor asked how they could overcome these limits. It became clear that overcoming them was connected to danger and when the person overcame them this could be considered *protean*. The students had to find the perceived features of a *Proteus*. It was not easy. They had to redefine their way of thinking. They presented features that could be considered positive.

So the *Proteus* was still a person who was different than the group but the norms that used to be negative became positive. The behaviour was considered weird and the individual was seen as rebelling against oneself. The students then had to recreate every aspect of this feature in a positive way. Students were involved while performing this task and the tutor's orders became clear for everyone. The students became familiar with the idea that being a *Proteus* does not have to be bad.

Summary

The three exercises were all different and the participants were not involved in the same way. The second task needed students to think only and in the first and third, they had to do something extra, (like painting). The students had to be much more involved while doing this. We think that addition of the artistic element made students more actively involved and also intellectually involved. They were then more willing to participate in discussions although some problems needed them to change their way of perceiving the world before they could do that.

Observation 3: Strategic management

Context

Place of observation: AHE.

Group studied: 4th year students of Management and Marketing, full-time studies. Men and women aged 24-25.

Researchers: Renata Figlewicz, Dorota Wodnicka

Dates of observation: 30 October 2003 6,13,20,27 November 2003 4, 11, 18 December 2003 8,16 January 2004

Thesis: The researcher can be a moderator in the dialogue between the teacher and the students.

The lecture-question format

The classes which we observed were in the form of a lecture. In most of them the lecturer presented new kind of problems and the students took notes in their notebooks. They knew at the beginning of the course that they would be obliged to describe strategic problems in a selected company on the basis of information they got from lectures, daily newspapers, the internet and hand-books.

All theoretical matters had been illustrated by examples from the daily life of enterprises and big companies. Students were in touch with these organisations in their everyday life, e.g. *Reserved* (they bought clothes there), *Era GSM* (some of them have mobile phones of this operator), etc.

To make it more active for the students the lecturer motivated them by asking questions. Students very often tried to guess the answers and they generally found more or less adequate answers and occasionally they struck home. After a few classes like this we proposed to the students and lecturer that they participate in some focus group based research.

Focus group activity

All of the students were warned that today's meeting would be spent on talks with external observers. Each of them agreed to sit in the circle with the researcher.

(R): What is the most effective way of learning for you?

(S1): I think examples are very important, not only giving the theory.

(S2): It is essential that these examples actually refer to contemporary companies.

(S3): The most effective way of learning is discussion.

(R): According to your opinion what does creative learning mean?

(S1): That everybody has their own opinion and can express himself.

(S2): Someone is finding the answer, thinking is most important.

(S3): Creative learning, that we can find the answers ourselves.

(S4) That we think more deeply, we try to ask more questions.

(S5) Yes, even if seven or more ideas are not appropriate it is important that but these ideas have already come into being, this is the creativity.

(R): Do you learn from each other?

(S1): Yes.

(R): What can you do to influence the process of learning, the mode of classes?

(S1): I try to ask questions but I don't always receive an answer, it depends on the professor.

(R): Can your attitude influence the course?

(S1): Yes, of course, if we ask and it is explained. We need to listen to influence on the course.

(R): What do we gain by introducing creativity in the classes?

(S1): Classes are more cool, there is a better atmosphere, better understanding and you get pleasure from coming to the classes.

(S2): Time passes faster, we get more. Even just looking at the notes we make a connection to the example. You do not have to learn it again later.

(S3): If the classes are run impersonally, it is difficult to read the notes at home.

(R): When is it possible to engage students in the didactic process?

(S1): It depends on the subject. Here we have some knowledge about this topic so it is easier to ask more.

(S2): It is not always easy to be cooperative during the classes.

(R): What do you mean?

(S1): We are sometimes told, "If you are not interested you can get out".

(S2): It is not possible to engage when the teacher puts up a barrier in the form or mode of their teaching.

(S3): This is when I do not like to engage in this kind of class.

(S4) I then have to write a mnemonic only, to remember it because I know I will need it to pass the exam.

(R): Does it mean that climate, atmosphere, and culture influence your learning?

(S1): If it is a poor atmosphere we will be afraid, we will not react, we will not be active.

(S2): If the lecture is with a large group it is very difficult to concentrate.

(S3): If the lecturer has a negative attitude towards the student it is more difficult but if the student really wants to learn something even then this person will not put him off.

(R): Have you got classes with foreign students?

(S1): When an interpreter is translating then everything is OK.

(S2): This class gives us a lot; it brings a quite different look, another perspective to our education.

(R): Has something new been created as the result of your participating in the class of strategic management?

(S1): We are now conscious of how different this class is to the normal.

(R): Are you the owners of knowledge, do you study for yourselves? For what are you studying?

(S1): To use it in life.

(S2): I study for myself, of course.

(S3): Notes are minor to me; they do not always reflect knowledge.

(S2): It would be cool if learning was a spontaneous process.

(R): What is the importance of this class for your personal development?

(S1): One may run a business for example, you never know what can be useful in life.

(S2): Everyone would like to manage own company, so it can be useful.

(R): What kinds of feelings and cognitive mechanisms are engaged in the class?

(S1): Getting our hands on the papers makes them more readable.

(S2): Excitement, the need to need to reach a truth, share an opinion, be inspired with another opinion.

(S3): Shyness, fear that something is wrong, at the beginning.

(R): What is the relationship between feeling and learning?

(S1): If I feel that I can ask I can learn more.

(S2): Support for future help.

(S3): If you feel that you are listened to, accepted, it influences your desire to participate in the classes. If someone disregards us, we do the same.

(R): How do you see yourselves as students?

(S1): We are the people who are using imagination and who own our experiences during the process of learning.

In the class following this focus group interaction the lecturer asks students more often about how they can communicate with each other in a more productive fashion. The students get some pleasure out of informing the teacher of the best way to communicate with them. You can see a clear co-operation within the group. The teacher is frequently at their side, even physically as he often sits with them at the desks. During the next class they will be engaged upon real business problems within their groups and we decided to film it.

Filmed Class Session

As always the students are garrulous before the class. The students will attempt to solve some case studies. There is a discussion about students' life between the teacher and the students. The teacher is claiming that it is the best part of their life. However, the students are complaining about future examination sessions and exams in general. By empathising with the students' problems the lecturer is becoming closer to them. He lets them know that he once was a student and understands their problems. The lecturer's empathy creates a very nice atmosphere and close relationships during the class. The fact that the teacher is participating with the students in the focus group, giving his own opinion on proposed topics means that he is much closer to the students. While they maintain an appropriate form of communication with him, respectful of his status, they still feel that the teacher is supporting them.

The lecturer introduces some problems, which could help students as they work individually on selected issues. The students are divided into two groups of five persons each. In one of them there are only girls working. In the second there are two boys. The students have got some materials from the lecturer and they start individual work. Very soon leaders are appointed in each group. They are organising the work, they write down solutions and we researchers film the class which exhibits interactions within the groups.

The students manage quite well with the case study and they do not require help from the lecturer. At the end of the exercise they all sit in a group with the teacher and talk about the solutions to the case studies. The discussion lasted into the break. It is very clear that the case studies are very interesting to the students.

Focus group follow up

During the next class we talked about what they felt and about their interactions in focus research. We tried to detect the most important moments in the process of learning.

We sit in a circle of students, lecturer and researchers. The second researcher filmed the group on a video camera. We start by introducing ourselves. One boy resists this way of starting the discussion but after stating that he is not obliged to talk about himself he responds that he was joking and introduces himself. It appears that this protest was because the students had become tired of this standard beginning. During their education at the university they had a lot of workshops on negotiation, integration and other similar aspects and they were bored with this manner of starting. We explain why it is important for us to know who we are talking with and of course, we introduced ourselves to let the students know something about us.

Further presentations from the focus group participants about themselves took place without any problems and some of the students talked with pleasure about themselves, about their plans for the future. The two Ukrainian girls point out that their objective for learning is very clear; to study, to get diplomas to have a better professional status. It becomes clear that it is the same in Poland and the Ukraine.

The students share, with pleasure, their opinion of the Strategic Management course. There were warm commentaries about the lecturer, as students compare this class with others. They pay particular attention to the way the teacher feels about his professional 'calling', his mission. They note how the teacher's personality can influence on their desire study and be cooperative. The most popular strategy for learning was using examples from daily life. Their study is very effective if they have to solve real problems.

They often they refer to the knowledge gained in other classes and recognise that it was only when the researchers came that they started to think about their role in the process of learning. They had not thought that they could cooperate with lecturers and co-realise classes, that they can be experts for lecturers by advising on learning strategy. The students as well as the lecturer agree that they have common goal.

It is suggested that they elaborate a common strategy of studying to make all classes more effective and that they should disseminate the success of this strategy for studying outcomes. They recognise that the responsibility for what they learn is theirs but often they feel ill-will from the teachers of other classes towards cooperation. They then act pragmatically so as not to waste time and if they want to know something from this subject they will have to work individually and be self reliant.

They are glad that the classes of strategic management are different. They recognise that this is due to the contribution of this teacher and his candidness concerning students' needs. They would like to have more teachers like him. They are not able to propose this kind of partnership and help in its realisation in classes of other lecturers. According to the students the initiative should come from the professors.

Summary

The students of the fourth year in the department of marketing and management already have opinions on classes. They express their opinions easily about the way of realising the type of classes they admire. Having completed three years of studies they can subjectively evaluate their own style of learning and the usefulness and efficacy of the classes concerned with their personal development and their future professional career. Most of the students have not yet had paid employment but the case studies make them able to use own experiences and observations. The essential element which enables interaction within the group and between students and lecturer was the temperament of the teacher.

However, in this case, the presence of the researchers resulted in a trial of elaborating a common strategy of learning. The presence of researchers caused that group to start actively co-operating with the teacher to develop a common setting for the best and most effective techniques of giving the classes. The students expressed a very clear desire to cooperate, with both researcher and teacher but they could not get rid of their sceptical belief that it is not possible with every teacher. They evaluated the cooperation with the lecturer as very good but they couldn't get rid of negative feelings expressed in comments about other subjects.

Using a focus group method of collecting the information about students' feelings towards the process of learning appears to be catalyst for co-operation from both the students and the teacher. A routine approach to teaching very often does not allow for dialogue between the teacher and the student to negotiate mutual relations in the process of education.

Conclusions

... Each observed subject group was different ...

In the first group the teacher took the leading role. In this group it appeared that teacher's intervention in the form of a focus survey resulted in interaction, understanding and co-operation between the students and the lecturer. The observers in this group acted as an accelerator producing dialogue. It was the teacher who, by asking questions, showed that it can be different, that dialogue is possible.

In the second group during the creative activity class it appeared that creative activity classes were characterised by the lowest degree of interaction. Students limited themselves to realising orders, but they also offered resistance towards proposed scenarios. Unsympathetic tutors influenced the stability of the group and the lack of speed of the classes.

In the third group the lecturer led the dialogue from the beginning and decided on the methods of transmission of the content. The focus survey showed the lecturer and students, that it was possible to negotiate a way of transmitting the contents of the programme; that if they had a common aim (education) they could work out a common strategy. They will develop this strategy and realise it during the semester. Focus group surveys and the presence of the teachers at these sessions changed the situation in the class a little. The teacher in this case acted as a moderator leading to a discussion about strategies of learning and teaching. Both students and tutors had interesting remarks about learning and teaching. In this group everyday creativity appeared important from the individual's point of view but it also had an influence on the environment.

References

Bielicka I., Olechnowicz H., Ślusarska-Kowalska Z, (1964) O klinicznym zastosowaniu metody malowania dziesięcioma palcami, *Psychologia Wychowawcza*, vol. 2

Jeffrey, B. and Woods, P. (2003) *The Creative School,* London: Routledge

Nęcka, E., Brocławik, K. (1984). O możliwościach wykorzystania synektyki w procesie rozwiązywania zadań wynalazczych, in Góralski, A. (ed.) *Zadanie, metoda, rozwiązanie. Techniki twórczego* myślenia. Z. 5. Warsaw: WNT

Nęcka, E (1995) *Proces twórczy i jego ograniczenia.* Kraków: Impuls

Nęcka, E. (2001) *Psychologia twórczo ci.* Gdansk: GWP

Osborn, A., F. (1959) *Applied imagination. Principles and procedures of creative thinking.* New York: Scribners

Woods, P., (1996) *Researching the art of teaching. Ethnography for educational use,* Rutledge, London and New York.

www.ingramcontent.com/pod-product-compliance
Lightning Source LLC
Chambersburg PA
CBHW020611270326
41927CB00005B/283